W9-BVO-608

BUDDHA PLAYS

18

2nd Edition

Instantly Improve Your Golf Game
Using Tips from the Great Master

Edward Sarkis Balian

Illustrations by Bonnie Bayham
Cover design by Danielle Cerceo

BUDDHA PLAYS 18

2nd Edition, 2nd Printing,
September, 2011
ISBN 978-0-9831181-3-8

SSP

Silver Sky Publishing, USA
Encinitas, California 92024
760-809-9778

www.BuddhaPlays18.com

Printed in the United States of America.

Dedicated to all the golfers of the world—
because you need all the help you can get

and

dedicated to all the non-golfers of the world—
because you are *truly* blessed.

FOR ONCE, A PREFACE
YOU REALLY SHOULD READ

Golf is the greatest game ever invented. Golf is also a very difficult game, and we all need all the help we can get. Why? Golf is a challenge that remarkably parallels life itself, probably more than any other sport ever created. In fact, that's what keeps us coming back to the course! So if golf is so much like life, can practical applications of Buddhist philosophy *significantly* improve your golf game? *Yes!*

Buddha Plays 18 is a unique golf instruction book. Unlike the hundreds of golf technique books on the market today, *Buddha Plays 18* gives insights and lessons mainly on the all-important *mental* side of the game.

But what can the over 2,500-year-old Buddha teach *you* about golf? Instead of just covering the theoretical "right way" to hit or putt a golf ball, Buddha shows you how to use your mind to create the shots and putts you want on the course.

While playing a round of golf, Buddha presents valuable stroke-saving instruction to pros and amateurs alike through the use of detailed visualizations (or "seeing in your mind's eye") and principles of Buddhist philosophy.

So come along with Buddha and his caddy as they play 18 at the fictitious Enlightenment Golf & Country Club set in sunny California. Learn from a true proven "Master" and put your powerful mental side to work in your golf game!

You'll learn about:

- The golden gutter technique
- Club selection dos and don'ts

(continued)

- Taking the fear out of bunkers, water and other hazards
- The "soul-plates" on your woods and hybrids and how to use them
- Spot-target golf
- The orange stake downswing technique
- How to, once and for all, buy the best putter on earth
- Golf course management throughout your round
- The three basic swing paths and what they do to your golf ball
- The shocking pink Mercury dime technique
- The very best practice tee preparation for your round
- The children's purple wading pool technique
- Exactly how to practice for best on-course results
- *...and so much more!*

Two little words comprise the load-bearing pillars of this book: *Suffering* and *Golf*. Talk about a hand-in-glove (or hand-in-golf glove, in this case) paradoxical relationship! Take a look at last Sunday's final round at the pro golf tournament of your choice. There was one happy winner kissing the trophy and 59 or more suffering golfers who were not kissing the trophy. Then you've got an additional 50 or more players who didn't even make the cut for the final rounds—they went home on Friday night even more miserable than all the other losers that Sunday. All totaled, that's a lot of suffering—and these players are the pros! So it almost goes without saying that the weekend amateur golfers of this world are even more over par on their respective scorecards of suffering.

To those who have never played the game, please just trust that at the International Hall of Fame for Suffering, the game of golf has an entire wing of its own built right on the premises.

Since you are reading this preface, odds are that you are already a fairly serious golfer. You've read a few books on the subject—maybe more than a few books. You already may know most or all of the classic swing mechanics including the usual dos and don'ts. In this book, Buddha will discuss many aspects of the golf swing and game, but he won't dwell on what's already in a million other instruction books such as various stances, postures, grips, keeping your head still, etc. Instead, Buddha's approach to your game improvement will go well beyond the mechanical moves. This is where you will find this book quite unique and different—but, I hope, extremely valuable. In Buddha's golf teachings, the correct mechanical moves will be coupled with an optimum state of awareness, focus and attitude, producing results that can be astounding on your future scorecards—really!

Since most of us are not professional golfers, we generally don't spend at least eight hours a day on the course six or seven days a week, so how can we ever significantly improve? Face it, most of us will never hit a Mickelson 330-yard drive or catapult Nicklaus-style, dead-on 1-iron approach shots. Now practice—the right type of practice—is very important at the range, but once you have the fundamentals down, the majority of your significant game improvement will come not from your physical approach to the game, but instead from your mental and attitudinal approach to the game.

Skeptical? Don't think golf is a game brimming with mental or attitudinal factors? *Ha!* Don't just take my word for it. Look at the 2010 U.S. Open at Pebble Beach and poor Dustin Johnson. In his own words, he was a totally different player from Saturday to Sunday, yet he was playing the identical course with the identical caddy, clubs, putter, ball, tees, shoes, hat and bag. That's just one sad example of immeasurable human suffering to be found throughout golf's colorful history.

Okay, so how does Buddha fit into this mess—did you find a hint in that last sentence? Buddhist philosophy is about eliminating suffering from life, so its segue into golf is obviously a no-brainer. Contrary to popular belief, though, Buddha is not a god. I won't hold that against him because I did just find out that he is a scratch golfer, and that's close enough to divinity for me.

No, Buddha is an ordinary person who found a way to reduce or eliminate suffering in life, and yes, in golf too. Wait a minute: An elimination of suffering? On a golf course? Do you have a pen handy? Where do I sign?

But first, let's look at who Buddha is not. He is not:

 A god

 A saint

 Superman in stylish sandals

 A leader of a religion (depending a bit on your definition of "religion")

 A Buddhist (at least not within his own recorded lifetime, since Buddhist philosophy only came into popular existence well after his death)

And while we're at it, Buddhists are not:

- People who set themselves on fire on a routine basis
- Necessarily strict vegetarians
- Only from India, Tibet or other faraway, mystical places
- Always dressed in orange robes
- Praying 14 hours a day
- Always sporting shaved heads
- Begging for donations at airports
- Always burning incense
- Seen dancing only to sitar music
- Sleeping only on beds of nails
- Despising all things in the Western world
- Perfect human beings

The Buddhist philosophy is for practical, everyday use. It is not just a set of dogmatic theories or chants to be memorized, sung about, or blindly followed. The point of Buddhism is to improve your life by reducing suffering in all your endeavors (yes, playing golf included) for the greater long-term good of both yourself and all humankind.

As luck would have it, today we're at the Enlightenment Golf & Country Club, and I'm considerably honored to be Buddha's caddy for his round. (I won the paper-stone-scissors contest between the caddies in the caddy shack to see who would carry for him!) And I can tell you right off that in writing this little book about our round together, Buddha's outlook and golf lessons have already changed things for me. So before you write off Buddha as an absurd golf instructor, know that just by researching and writing this book, my golf game, after 45 years of scorecard-documented suffering, has significantly improved. No kidding.

How? Fair question. Among other things, I've developed a much stronger pre-shot routine and now have far better focus, concentration, patience and humor, coupled with vivid pre-shot visualizations, swing-thoughts, and more.

I've also noticed my improved attitude in little, everyday things, like how I treat my loved ones, talk to total strangers, behave better in infamous I-405 L.A. traffic jams, open doors for old folks, and extend patience to a greater level than I ever thought I was capable of. I've even kind of surprised myself—the stuff discussed in this little book really does work, both on the golf course and on that other great golf course (also filled with lateral hazards) called "life."

I hope you enjoy this little book—I know it can improve your game!

ACKNOWLEDGEMENTS

I wish to thank those involved in the completion of *Buddha Plays 18*. Thanks to Dr. Ron Lake and Karen Silsby for their content review and insights regarding Buddhist philosophy.

Judith Balian is thanked for her work with final text editing, numerous illustration scans, graphics and website construction.

Thanks are extended to Danielle Cerceo for the front and back cover artwork and to Bonnie Bayham for all illustrations within the book. Appreciation is also extended to Denise Olaguer for the initial draft word processing and to Cheryl Corey and Stephanie Reedy for their assistance in the printing of this second edition.

Thanks also to the kind staff at Encinitas Ranch Golf Course, Encinitas, California. I spent countless (and enjoyable) hours on their golf course and practice range as I outlined and refined the instruction and tips suggested in this book.

Thanks to three of my favorite golf buddies over the past 30 years, Marty Martlock, Vic Meyers and Jay Lotoski, as they provided much of the inspiration behind this book. We played a lot of rounds together and even enjoyed the mis-hits! Now *that's* true friendship.

Heartfelt gratitude to all—may you hit them long and straight as you walk all of life's bountiful fairways!

Edward Sarkis Balian, Ph.D.
Encinitas (San Diego), California
September, 2011
(2nd Edition, 2nd Printing)

INTRODUCTION

Buddha's Got Game!

Buddha's golf game is about concentration, consistency, relaxation, and a total awareness of his next shot. He practices both the physical and mental parts of the game. He is not about macho strength, Mulligans, swearing at his golf ball, or impressing all those around him. While he understands and practices excellent swing mechanics, he plays great golf mainly by using the basic principles of Buddhist philosophy. This includes, among other things, consistent use of precise and powerful visualizations. More on this later, throughout the book.

On the golf course, Buddha is not particularly long, especially for a formidable scratch golfer. As mentioned, he is not about brute strength or trying to muscle the ball. In fact, you might be surprised to find that you may even hit the ball farther than he does—but I doubt you could beat him on the course!

Buddha uses off-the-rack metal woods and traditional, forged blades. His shaft flex is "regular" and his set is consistently swing-weighted to D-2. He swings slowly, producing a relatively low club head speed (typically a 94 mph driver swing), but his ball striking is usually dead on the sweet spot of each club. He hits a tour-standard 3-piece ball with, predictably for him, plenty of "feel." He has a dynamite short game and is a well-above-average putter.

Compare your club distances to Buddha's typical yardages:

Driver......270 yards
3-wood.....240
5-wood.....220
3-iron.......190
4-iron.......180

```
5-iron.......170
6-iron.......160
7-iron.......150
8-iron.......140
9-iron.......130
PW 48*.....10-120
SW 56*.....10-90
LW 60*.....10-60
```
Wood-shafted blade putter (from the 1920s)

As for attire, Buddha looks sharp today in his loose-fitting traditional orange monk's robe. His sandals are specially fitted with golf spikes secured by Super Glue.

Buddha is right-handed for today's round, not to take anything away from Phil Mickelson or all the other lefties in the world. (Heck, some of my best golf buddies, including my cool son-in-law, are lefties!) Actually, Buddha can shoot par or better from either side of the ball.

Buddha Warms Up at the Practice Tee

For today's round at the Enlightenment Golf & Country Club, Buddha begins his driving range session with a gentle yoga stretching routine. He tells me that when he went to the range for the very first time as a young boy he was amazed at how the place provided free green AstroTurf yoga mats at every practice tee. He recalled thinking, "Cool! I love this game already!"

His morning yoga practice consists of repeated deep breathing combined with a few of the more common yoga postures including sun salutations, downward dog, and tree pose. Buddha claims that any decent golfer knows the critical importance of stretching. Then he reminds me about the deeper goal of yoga, connecting the body to the mind, this being so central to successful golf (and life).

Next Buddha starts hitting a few practice balls, beginning with his pitching wedge, on up through his bag, and then back to his sand and lob wedges for some short pitches and chips. I watch with interest as he visualizes each shot beforehand, then tries to place his hit ball at the precise location where he's pictured it in his mind's eye. His actual swing and hits are only the mechanical part of the effort—important, but only the physical part of the game.

Predictably, his swing is tension-free, very loose and very full. It appears to me that he actually savors every moment of his swing, from take-away to follow-through. I see no tension or "pressing" anywhere along his swing path or in his hand action. No macho here at all. He is deliberate, confident, slow, and steady. He hits slight draws and gentle fades at will. In just watching him for a few minutes, I'm already impressed by what he's doing and not doing on the practice range. He's not trying to annihilate the ball. He's not cursing every other shot. He's not in a big rush to hit through his practice bucket. He doesn't empty out his bucket onto the ground; instead he purposely goes back to the bucket to pick out each ball, one at a time, explaining that this slows him down. He picks a spot target before each shot. He's not just hitting ball after ball aimlessly. And he is not just hitting driver, but instead working slowly through his entire bag.

Buddha concludes his practice session by taking a cross-legged sitting (lotus) position on the driving range yoga mat. He goes into his morning meditation. The practice of meditation is at the core of Buddhist philosophy, so I assume we'll see what role this actually plays in a golf game later on today. As he meditates, Buddha is obviously doing some deep breathing and appears extremely serene.

When was the last time you saw someone on a driving range mat meditating before their round? Yeah, okay, to say the least I guess Buddha's driving range practice routine may seem a tad eccentric—but I, for one, can't wait to see this guy tee off.

Buddha's Practice Tee Tips

- Stretch all your muscles out: neck, forearms, wrists, upper chest, hips, knees and legs.

- Do deep breathing exercises; hold your concentration on a peaceful scene.

- Hit all the clubs in your bag, starting with wedges then moving up through the bag.

- Swing every club as if it were an 8-iron (more on this later).

- Keep your head down and steady, and follow-through high and complete.

- Hit no more than three balls with each club, then move to the next club in the bag.

- As you move to a new club, take practice swings before you hit balls.

- Hit to a practice flag target every time.

- Aligned with your practice flag target, pick a spot target about one yard in front of you for each and every practice shot; align to this spot, not the flag. Your ball should start its flight on this line.

- Try subtle grip experiments for fades and draws; keep careful track of what you are doing as you will get different results.

- For each shot, check the direction of your divot; analyze it and relate it to your spot target and ball flight.

- Accurately establish your average distances for each club.

- Tee-up 3-4-5 woods, hybrids and long irons very low to help avoid pulling the ball.

- Write reminders or mantras on the soleplates of each club; read and focus on them as you pull clubs out of your bag (more on this later).

- Slow down *everything* you are doing, including your swing.

Okay, are you currently doing even one or two on the above list? Yeah, I thought so, me too.... Hmm...just by observing Buddha, we might already be learning a little—and we haven't even started the round yet! I've already decided that I'll be way better off doing a lot more listening and observing than talking during the next 18 holes. As Buddha's caddy for today —I must be living right to get this gig—I grab his very plain and simple maroon golf bag, and we head toward the first tee.

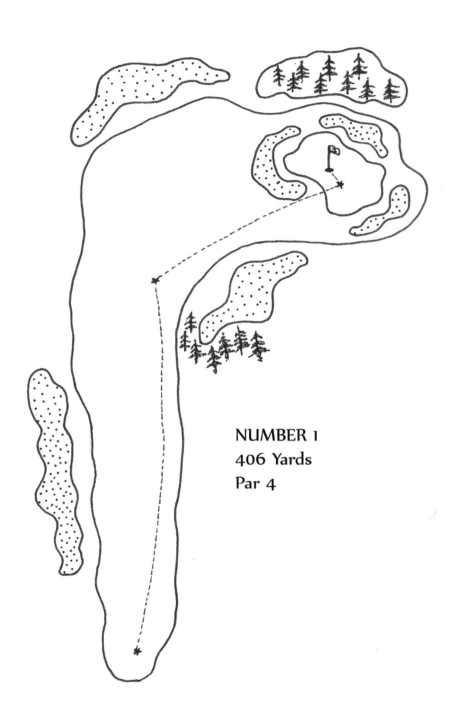

NUMBER 1
406 Yards
Par 4

NUMBER 1
406 Yards, Par 4

Caddy's View from the Tee:

A dogleg right, not long, but a fairly wide fairway sloping left-to-right) toward the dogleg curve, then leading to an extremely wide green framed with deep sand bunkers. Stay left of the trees just at the dogleg knee. Watch club selection as the bunker straight out is in play, only 248 from the tee. Just take it easy on Number 1 and stay out of trouble. Most important: It's the first tee—try to keep your adrenaline under control!

Man, is this every golfer's (and caddy's) dream or what? The sun is just now rising into a fresh California morning sky. I'm standing behind Buddha at the Number 1 tee box at the Enlightenment Golf & Country Club. I pinch myself—am I really here? A few seconds pass as I experience the awe of this surreal moment. Meanwhile, we've already drawn a respectful five-deep gallery around us as everyone wants to see the great Buddha slam a whopping 350-yard Mickelson-style opening drive. But that is not to be.

Buddha breaks the quiet sunrise moment with, "3-wood, please."

3-wood off the tee? Whaaat? Not a driver? Well, all right. I guess he knows what he's doing. As caddy, I complete my first official job duty by handing him his club of choice.

Buddha turns and comments to the gallery that Buddhist philosophy is about recognizing, then eliminating suffering. He says there are Four Noble Truths. Logically, Buddha begins with the First Noble Truth of Buddhism: Life is *suffering* (or *Dukkha*). And hitting a long drive from the tee here may well create *plenty* of suffering, especially for those who are self-absorbed, impatient, and greedy for distance.

Next he says that recognizing that the mere *desire* for things (including greed or lust for more driving distance), is the Second Noble Truth. Desiring things we want or having a desire for self over all else (the widespread "it's all about me" behaviors) are constantly working against our long-term happiness. These "attachments" as Buddha calls them, just keep feeding our suffering. So translated to golf talk: If I clobber a 350-yard drive with my new $400 hi-tech club, I can impress everyone at the 1st tee and be cool in life. Not.

Despite what the gallery wants to see from him, Buddha chooses to hit a shorter 3-wood drive with a slight draw (right-to-left ball direction). He says, "Keep your thinking simple, and don't let your ego or what others think you are supposed to do influence you."

Buddha pauses, takes a relaxing deep breath and smacks a gorgeous 240-yard 3-wood draw down the right side of the fairway. He gives me a quick wink and whispers over, "'Hit 'em long and straight' may be one of the oldest golf adages, but it's just not always true. You don't always need brute strength or straight direction in life. Instead, the situation here demanded that one must harness physical strength and hit a draw for the greater, deeper good."

He continues, "Just like in life, the best direction for you may not be the one everyone else expects you to take. Golf has straight shots, slices, fades, draws, and hooks. You can get from A to B in many different ways. The curved routes which usually involve more challenge, adventure, or skill may often be wiser than taking the direct route. Sometimes you have choices in direction and sometimes not.

"It's also important to keep your mind serene, steady, and in the present moment. Forget about impressing people who happen to be watching you in the great golf gallery of life. Instead, stay focused on what makes sense in the situation for the greater good—this applies in *any* situation, including the 1st tee.

"Acting on the expectations of others—like those in the gallery wanting me to hit it long and straight—can be a big mistake in life, even though those people may be fine folks and very well-intended. My shorter distance, draw drive was much wiser in this situation. Wisdom is the result of experience, and it all leads to happiness—and ultimately to enlightenment."

We walk out to his ball sitting up nicely in the fairway as Buddha continues, "The Third Noble Truth says that if the cause of suffering lies in our selfish desires, then we obviously need to overcome those cravings to find our happiness. So by recognizing that selfish desire is our own downfall, we can start work toward eliminating it."

I reply, "Okay, I kind of get it so far, but I'm far from sold. These first three Noble Truths seem unmotivating, uninspired, ill-founded, and even bizarre! How would I ever convince myself to *not* want to hit a 350-yard drive?"

Buddha chuckles and remarks, "The Fourth Noble Truth speaks to just that question. It's all in what's called the Eightfold Path. That is the only way 'out' of our suffering and our way 'in' to happiness and ultimately, enlightenment— as well as better golf!"

Buddha promises to tell me more about this so-called Eightfold Path at appropriate points during today's round, but only if I'm ready to hear it. He claims that while it's powerful stuff, the teacher can do little if the student is not ready to watch or listen. (Hmm…this rings true regarding that video swing lesson I took yesterday from my local PGA teacher. Did I really look as bad as the camera showed when I was hitting golf balls? No way! That camera lens must have been dirty or malfunctioning!)

Buddha now sets up for his second shot on this opening par 4. He hits a relaxed 135-yard 8-iron faded into the green. It's a sweet, soft landing. Nice.

Now on the green, Buddha's putt gently curves left into the side of the cup. Birdie 3!

Well okay, even after one hole I must admit that there's something intriguing and different about what I've heard and seen so far. But I'm far from convinced that the Four Noble Truths have anything to do with anything. Can this Eastern world, philosophical "blue (incense) smoke" really work for me— especially on a *golf course?* On the other hand, Buddha just birdied Number 1. Not bad. I guess he must know *something.*

BUDDHA'S CORNER
ON THE FOUR NOBLE TRUTHS

The Four Noble Truths of Buddhist Philosophy as applied to your golf game are:

 Suffering exists in golf—oh brother, no argument here!

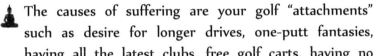 The causes of suffering are your golf "attachments" such as desire for longer drives, one-putt fantasies, having all the latest clubs, free golf carts, having no foursomes in front of you, wanting the wind at your back on every number, etc.

 Eliminating your golf-oriented desires (or "attachments") will eliminate your golf suffering.

 Following and practicing the Eightfold Path will eventually and ultimately eliminate your golf attachments. It is the *only way* out of this mess and into full membership at the Enlightenment Country Club where every shot you take will be a hole-in-one. Well...sort of...more on this later!

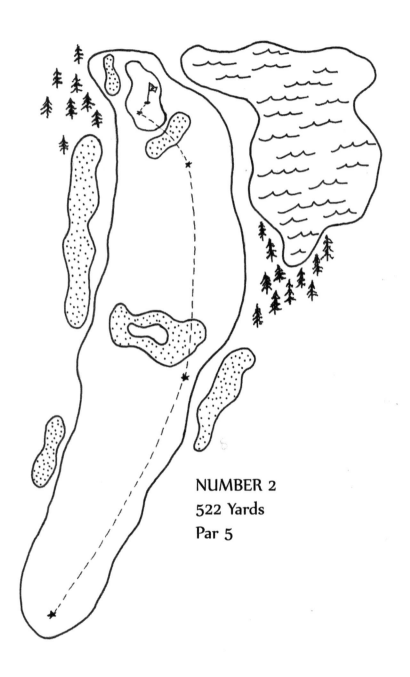

NUMBER 2
522 Yards
Par 5

NUMBER 2
522 Yards, Par 5

Caddy's View from the Tee:

The fairway is lined with sand bunkers right, left, and across the landing area. Distance combined with accuracy is a must here— and a tough combination to execute. The left side fairway bunker goes half the length of the fairway. Trees and water are right. A giant sand bunker is about ten yards in front of the green. To add to the potential suffering, the green is very narrow with deep bunkers right and back-left. Don't miss left or you're in the pine trees.

At 522 yards, this hole will be a long journey. I've got a funny feeling that I'm going to learn a lot on this hole. This time, Buddha calls for driver. He stands behind the tee and visualizes or "sees" exactly where he wants his ball to land. He concentrates and relaxes, breathing deeply.

His swing is slow, buttery smooth and sweeping. Whack! Away the little white ball flies, hanging like a tiny round kite against the sky. It's a very slight draw of about 265 yards, ending just at the right edge of this pristine fairway. Trying to be a sociable caddy, I comment as we walk up the fairway, "You're obviously really into the mental part of your game."

"What other part is there?" he quickly replies. Hmm, this sets me thinking again. This stuff is nothing if not high-minded; it's not for everyone.

THE EIGHTFOLD PATH

Buddha picks up the earlier conversation, "The Eightfold Path leads us out of suffering. It is comprised of these eight principles: Right Speech, Right Livelihood, Right Thought, Right Effort, Right Concentration, Right Action, Right Mindfulness and Right

Knowledge. I will use them *all* in today's round; in fact, I already started using them back on the first hole."

"But what do these phrases actually mean? *How* do you use them?" My inquiring mind wants to know.

Buddha replies, "You'll see, in time—*if you are ready* to see them." Standing behind the ball for his second shot, Buddha sizes up his prospects. A crummy lie confronts him. Bad luck? I sense that he is tempted to curse like the rest of us, but he does not. Instead he just laughs at what appears to be the ill fate of the bad lie. He quickly shakes off the situation and hits a perfect 5-wood draw that lays him up as planned, in the fairway just short of the right greenside bunker. Have *you* ever hit a 5-wood draw from a bad lie? Wow— nice shot!

We're walking up to Buddha's ball for his third shot when a fan from the gallery heckles, "Man, don't use that wedge; use your 9-iron instead." Disregarding this external "advice," Buddha's third shot, with his wedge, gets him within three feet of the hole for an uphill birdie attempt. He easily putts out, stroking it strong into the center of the cup. He doesn't even look up from the putt— he knows this one is in the hole from the instant he strokes it. A second textbook bird for the man in the orange robe!

Now average golfers might score a 7 here, say 6, and write down 5. And Number 2 might be the perfect place to do exactly that. In Buddha's case, why not write down an eagle 3 on the scorecard instead of his true birdie 4?

But Buddha speaks clearly about Right Speech, one of the eight principles in the Eightfold Path, "Right Speech transgressions include lying, cursing, and talking too much. The former need no further explanation and the latter is exemplified when other golfers give unsolicited swing advice. Thanks to the innately frustrating nature of the game, these Right Speech infractions are typical behaviors of almost every golfer found on every golf course around the world. Any argument? No, I didn't think so."

I chime in, "Okay, so let's talk solutions. What *should* happen when we don't want to own up to the true score we shot on a hole?" Buddha explains that attachment to anything (including our golf scores) only leads to more suffering. Understanding that your golf score is an unnecessary attachment is a step toward eliminating your suffering. So why lie about your score? It's quite counterproductive to your game as Buddha sees it. Said another way, lying about your golf score will only make you a *worse* golfer.

Okay, how about when we curse at a golf ball? (And don't tell me you've never done it!) Buddha insists that this will only lead to yet more suffering. He claims that developing a strong mental discipline will improve your game tremendously. I must admit that he must be right as I've never seen a golf ball obey any of my angry outbursts, especially not my profane, angry outbursts!

Buddha says that one excellent antidote to anger and profanity is humor. Are we all maybe taking this old Scottish game just a bit too seriously? Indeed. According to Buddha, by laughing at yourself, relaxing and recapturing some inner peace instead of getting mad and cursing, you just might play that next shot better. And there is always a next shot. Case in point on this hole: Buddha shook off his bad lie and hit a great second shot with his 5-wood. I was there. I saw it.

And what about that fan who rudely and loudly voiced his opinion about which club Buddha should hit? When it comes to giving golf advice, Buddha says just to hold off on giving it unless you are asked. In short, hold your tongue on unsolicited advice and instead place your energy into *your own* behavior instead. Simple isn't it? But we all know that holding back our tongues is not always so easy.

As we walk to the next tee, Buddha continues, "Right Livelihood is another of the eight principles. This has much to do with our round today since my activity as a golfer is only a vehicle for my teaching of Buddhist philosophy. Hence, my livelihood as a teacher is noble and right. I'm not making a living by trying to scam people over the Internet or something. It's important to be of service to the world. And golf itself can be a fine livelihood so long as you don't sandbag your handicap!"

He reminds me that Right Speech and Right Livelihood are just two of the principles in the Eightfold Path; there are six more to come. And all the principles he's going to tell me about must be *practiced*, just like your golf swing at the driving range.

But here's the good news: He claims the payoff from all your practice will be super-sized. Get this: Buddha says that as you practice the Eightfold Path you will find a deeper knowledge of self, and as your inner serenity and wisdom *in*crease, your golf scores will *de*crease. He guarantees it.

I don't know about you, but that's good enough for me, coming from a guy who is *already 2-under par after only two holes!*

BUDDHA'S CORNER
Two Elements of the Eightfold Path

ON RIGHT SPEECH

The legendary Arnold Palmer penalized himself when his 5-iron inadvertently touched his ball during address. It cost him a tournament, but gained him incalculable integrity that's been associated with him throughout his spectacular career, now spanning over 60 years.

Right Speech, one of the eight Eightfold Path principles, includes among other things, the avoidance of telling lies. Buddha claims that lying can never actually lead to better golf. He believes we need to put our mental energies into far more positive thoughts and actions—and that this will lead to both a better golf game and a better life too!

Other Right Speech examples include not talking to disturb your playing partners and being sure to loudly call out "fore" to warn others of a stray shot.

ON RIGHT LIVELIHOOD

PGA teachers make an honorable living by giving instruction to golfers---teachers try to eliminate suffering and this is Right Livelihood indeed.

Are "honest livings" made by the diabolical 7,700-yard golf course architects? (Hmm...Buddha's going to have to think that one over.)

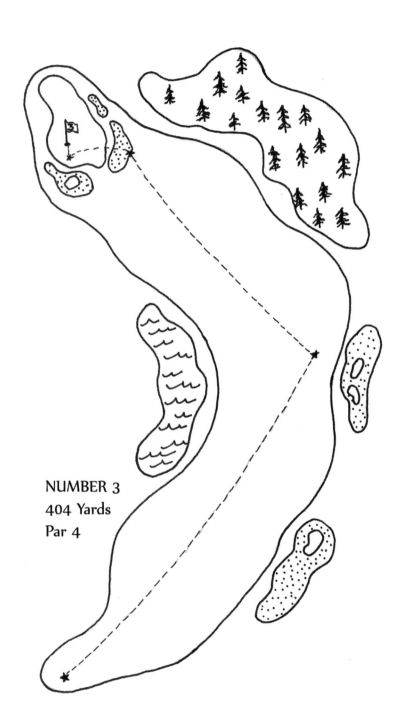

NUMBER 3
404 Yards
Par 4

NUMBER 3
404 Yards, Par 4

From the back tee Buddha sends a low trajectory driver into the right-to-left wind. The ball draws beautifully with the dogleg left and comes to rest about 260 yards out on the right edge of the fairway.

Nice shot by the man draped in orange. While putting his club back into his bag, I notice some strange notations on the soleplate (or underside) of Buddha's driver. The scrawled letters read:

"8-I," "EDS" and "THRU."

Puzzled, I ask him what they mean. Buddha explains, "These are 'mantras.' Mantras are words, phrases, or acronyms whose repetitions create a spiritual connection for me. The '8-I EDS' stands for 'hit every club as if it were an 8-iron and with an Easy Down-Swing' and the 'THRU' is to help me remember to create a full and high follow-through of my swing in my mind's eye. Taking the time to review these mantras, especially before a swing with my longer clubs, helps slow me down and put a better swing path on the ball.

"I write these mantra words on the bottom of my club. I call that spot the 'soul plate' of my driver. Get it?" He giggles. "During meditation or at any other time, even right now, repeating a mantra either out loud or silently—or even just seeing it in written form— clears my mind and relaxes me. Mantras are especially powerful during my meditation sessions on the practice range or on a tee. From a state of total serenity I can more easily 'see' my easy swing and my full follow-through—and this automatically improves my game."

Hold it right there. Did I hear, "*Automatically* improves my game?" It's that easy? Sign me up!

For his second shot, with about 144 remaining to the flagstick, Buddha calls for his 7-iron. He hits a bit of an ill surprise, a hanging fade into the wind and comes up well short and into the right greenside sand bunker. Ah-ha! This man is *not* infallible after all! Actually, as his mere mortal caddy, I suddenly feel a bit relieved and ask, "So what happened there? I figured you for no mistakes after all that mantra talk."

Buddha replies, "Between the two of us, I'm afraid that you're the only one who is expecting me to be perfect."

But the gallery too is stunned at Buddha's mis-hit. As we approach the sand bunker, a young kid sneers from the gallery, "Hey Boode, you really blew that one—you don't look so red hot to me. My 75-year-old Grandma Mabel could have hit a 7-iron better than that!"

Defending my boss, I lose my cool and snap back, "Hey, why don't you zip it before I jam this mashie down your throat?"

Buddha softly whispers to me, "That is not Right Speech. Why yell back? When you fight fire with fire, you end up with nothing but ashes.

"Remember that Right Speech is one of the Eightfold Path principles. And while I'm back on that subject, note that my *wrong* actions in my last swing led me *into* the trouble, but some new Eightfold Path *right* actions are going to get me *out* of this trouble. Right Thought, also known as my intentions and visualizations, enable me to 'see' myself getting out of the bunker. And if I can really see it happen, it will happen.

"Right Concentration will provide the sharp focus to my visualized picture. I must hold the visualized picture in my mind and keep it sharply focused, never murky.

"Right Mindfulness is a way of thinking that keeps me in the present moment. I'm not thinking about the previous shot that got me into the trouble. I'm not thinking about the prior holes I've already played. I'm not thinking about the next tee. I'm not thinking about my mother-in-law who is coming to visit next weekend. I'm only thinking about this next shot and no other.

"You know, it's not the errors that are important. It's in *how you recover* from those errors that's important. In fact, an error is nothing more than a new opportunity. There really are no mistakes or mis-hits.

"Along those lines, recognize that the Eightfold Path principles are commonly used together in a sort of harmony. They are the most powerful when used in combination." With that, totally unbothered and serene, Buddha splashes out of the bunker with his 56-degree sand wedge to within five feet. He sinks the right-to-left putt with his ancient-looking, wood-shafted putter. Even though he obviously mis-hit his earlier 7-iron, he taught me something. He totally forgot about his bad shot immediately and recovered from his "error" in excellent fashion.

Buddha summarized his play on this hole very candidly, "I was a bit out-to-in on my 7-iron swing path with an open face, and that, of course, put fade spin on the ball, which is what I wanted to do. But my distance was a bit shorter than I expected as a result of the fade, so I caught the right sand trap. It should have been an easy play, but I just messed up. And 'trap' is not the best word either. Instead, think of it as a sand 'opportunity!'" Now that's an interesting way to look at it, I must admit.

Hmm. Right Thought, Right Concentration, and Right Mindfulness. So here are three more of the eight principles in the

Eightfold Path. Added to Right Speech which Buddha discussed earlier, we've heard four of the Eightfold Path principles so far.

I notice that Buddha's thinking and actions never seem disjointed, but rather always interrelated. And this "living in the present moment" (or Right Mindfulness stuff as he calls it) seems to be really important. After a bad shot, like his second shot here with the 7-iron, Buddha just forgot about it and moved forward. As golfers, we know that forgetting about a bad shot is far easier said than done, but Buddha just showed us that it definitely is possible. After all, he did just save par, so how wrong can he be?

Through three, Buddha is still two-under par—pretty darn impressive.

BUDDHA'S CORNER
A Third Element of the Eightfold Path

THREE

ON RIGHT THOUGHT

Gene Sarazen invented the sand wedge and brought compassionate relief to millions of golfers! Gene was flying with Howard Hughes when he observed the moving flaps on Hughes' plane lift the aircraft skyward. Through Sarazen's problem-solving, he creatively visualized, designed and successfully implemented the very first sand wedge, using the idea of leading edge 'lift.' Buddha calls Sarazen's creative problem solving and visualizing a fine example of Right Thought.

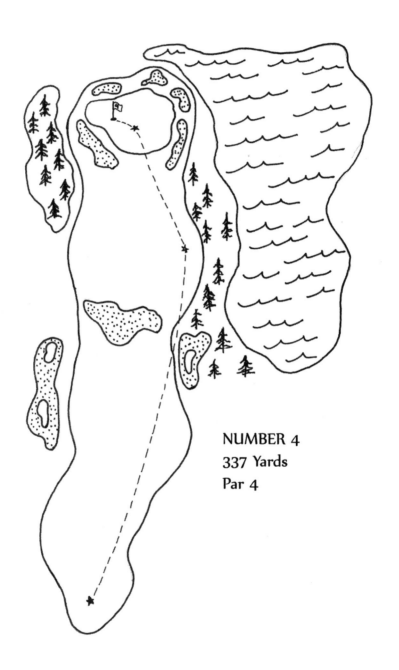

NUMBER 4
337 Yards
Par 4

NUMBER 4
337 Yards, Par 4

Caddy's View from the Tee:

Fear. Just looking out at those eight (!!!) ominous bunkers makes me fearful. Water is to the right and should be out of play, but the strong prevailing right-to-left winds are not. Don't get cute and go too far right off the tee—you may never get out of trouble. On the approach, get your pin distance exact—and don't pull it left into the woods. Big time caution is needed: Don't let that short yardage mislead you.

Trying to be a good caddy, I advise Buddha, "*Eight* sand bunkers here, count 'em. And a tough right-to-left wind off the water is really gusting. You better protect your round and back off on this tee shot—maybe even hang way back with a 6-iron lay-up."

Ha! My caddy advice seems to stink again. Buddha is having none of it. Instead he puts an angelic swing on his 5-wood and with a huge draw, blisters the ball 230 yards. It lands at the right edge of the fairway, well short of that intensely evil-looking, right greenside bunker. "Why go right?" I ask. Buddha explains that he wanted to carefully go into the green from the right. The 5-wood gave him accuracy and enough distance. He's going to count on his short game from about 110 yards in—a good strategy to be sure.

"But what about hitting that 5-wood so high in this wind?" I inquire.

"You know it's amazing how little the wind affects a good hit," Buddha replies. You know, I've noticed that at the driving range sometimes myself. I think Buddha's right about this too. I remember that no less than Ben Hogan also commented about how little the wind affected a well-hit ball.

But did Buddha's 5-wood tee shot go *exactly* where he wanted it? Buddha says, "No, I was really trying to draw it a bit more left, giving me a more open play to this tiny green. As it turns out, I'm a bit too far right, and now I've got another of life's little challenges ahead of me. I'm going to have to deal with that right greenside bunker after all. This was not really my grand plan from the tee, but life is full of unexpected turns. This is one of them, so I'll deal with it. Don't expect to *control* everything. In fact, don't expect to control *anything*. Just let go of your expectations or attachments, use the Eightfold Path principles, and do your best."

With a right-to-left wind off the water continuing to further complicate things, Buddha goes on to tell me that he now will now hit a soft pitching wedge fade into that wind and literally curve his ball around that nasty right bunker. *And* the fade spin will quickly—very quickly—stop the ball upon its soft-landing on the green. *And* he will leave the ball short of the hole to give himself a far easier uphill, as opposed to downhill, putt. (Whew, did you get all that? I'm not entirely sure I did, and I'm his caddy, for crying out loud!)

Buddha is using what he calls Right Effort. He holds only positive attitudes and uses positive swing thoughts. He says, "As I go into my take away I think 'slow and smooth.' At my start down, my swing thought is to gently hammer down an 'orange colored stake' that I visualize as just back behind my right pocket. At impact, my swing thought is to just come through the ball to a full follow-through and pretend that I'm swinging a very easy 8-iron. I'm just swinging freely, and the ball happens to be in the way."

Buddha studies this situation very peacefully yet carefully, pitching wedge in hand. I can almost feel his kinetic energy. Yet, at the same time, he seems strangely calm and relaxed. His pre-swing routine is flawless. His practice swing is a thing of artistic beauty. I can imagine his Right Thought (visualization), Right

Concentration (sharp focus) and Right Mindfulness (being in the present moment), but my knees are shaking just at the thought of this impending shot. All of a sudden, it seems like the wind off the bay just got worse. What would Palmer's hand strength would do here? Nicklaus' driving leg power? Player's incredible short-game finesse? How would Babe Zaharias, Wright, or Lopez handle this situation? And what will Buddha's inner strength do here?

In the image of the Babe, Buddha steps up and lays on about the smoothest swing I've ever seen put on a golf ball, complete with a fluid, high follow-through. He's well up high and over the bunker, soft lands, but, due to the head wind, he does leave it well short of the hole. Under the circumstances, still a spectacular shot, but he leaves a lot of work for himself on the putting green. I am a bit disappointed but again reminded that Buddha is not supernatural. He is not a god. He is an ordinary guy—who's shooting-under par!

The putt? A 10-footer, uphill, right-to-left. Buddha sinks it dead center for another birdie. Great putt.

In retrospect, as Buddha's caddy I was honestly consumed with fear for him as I stood at the tee and looked at those eight sand bunkers. Buddha later explained to me that "sand bunker" is just silly golf jargon. He says that no truly confident golfer ever worries about sand and reiterates that we should replace the bunker or trap terminology with "sand *opportunity*." Giving credit where credit is due, he adds, "Thanks to Sarazen's invention of the wedge, the sand shot has become one of the easiest shots in all of golf. Basically it's not about sand at all. It's all about *fear,* alive and well, and existing only in the golfer's mind."

I guess we can view all this Buddhist talk with some healthy skepticism, but we're now three-under par after four holes, and I'm becoming a bit of a believer. It's still early though, and this *is* golf, after all.

Visualize the orange stake well behind and to the right
of your pocket and gently hammer it down on your
downswing; this will force your right shoulder *down
and in* instead of spinning it outward toward the ball
on your downswing. Try it!

BUDDHA'S CORNER
A Fourth Element of the Eightfold Path

ON RIGHT EFFORT

Hold only positive swing thoughts like hammer down the "orange stake" and complete an "easy down swing" and "high follow-through." Be sure to use these swing thoughts and images on every single shot. Until you feel fully confident about the shot you are about to make and can "see" those swing images clearly in your mind, don't even start your backswing.

ON FEAR

Fear is not going to ruin Buddha's journey, either in a round of golf or in a round of life. Fear is another form of attachment. He just doesn't accept delivery.

ON BUNKERS OR TRAPS

Forget the words bunker or trap. Instead call them "opportunities." With the right attitude and the right tool (a sand wedge), you can meet the challenges.

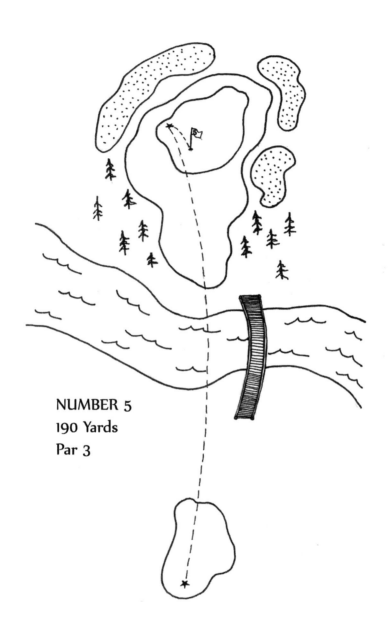

NUMBER 5
190 Yards
Par 3

NUMBER 5
190 Yards, Par 3

We arrive at the 5th tee and the wind is swirling. Buddha gives a long look to this par 3 and asks for his 3-iron. After his usual mental disciplined pre-shot routine, he hits a high draw away from the trouble on the right. The height on his shot, not easy to achieve with a 3-iron, helps the ball stick on the green. He leaves himself a 15-foot putt with a severe left-to-right break. This is going to be a real pressure putt.

As we walk up towards the green, I sense that this might be a fitting time to ask Buddha about the fine art of putting, certainly one of golf's most important, but often frustrating, aspects. I comment about the fact that there are literally thousands of putter designs: Blades. Mallets. Hi-tech. wood shafted. Low-tech. Offsets. Non-offsets. Face balanced. And on and on. If there ever were a more confusing array of tools to accomplish a single task in life, I've never seen it. So what really makes for a good putter, anyway? Gee, why not get a timely and inspired Eastern world opinion on the subject?

Buddha replies by starting with a discussion concerning, of all things, meditation. He claims that meditation is sadly misunderstood by the Western world—and yet we Westerners need it badly. Buddha explains that the one central goal of meditative practice is the calming of the mind. In meditation he concentrates (or focuses) on a visualization (or picture) in his mind of serenity.

Okay, so what does that mean? He says that the true power of visualization or "seeing things in your mind's eye" can seem quite daunting and other worldly to a novice, but it just takes practice. Lots of practice.

Right Concentration (focus) leads into Right Thought (visualization) and they work hand in hand in this case. Buddha points out that the awesome power of Right Concentration and Right Thought are already on loan to athletes everywhere—it's not really anything new to the world of sports. To drive home his point, he asks, "Do you think an Olympic figure skater sees herself leaping up, spinning, then falling to the ice? Do you really believe that Ted Williams saw mental pictures of himself taking a called third strike as he went on to bat .344 lifetime? Never!"

Buddha goes on, "Apply the same thinking to putters. The best putter for you will be one which most easily allows you to sharply 'see' the ball path going to the cup. In my own case, the putter head must help create what I call my imaginary 'golden gutter' which my ball will channel through when putt. I paint the gutter gold in my mind so I can visualize it more clearly. This golden gutter is the exact width of my putter head. The gutter even extends a few inches behind my ball, going back and through. That additional visualization detail helps me take the putter back square to my putting line, which is essential to placing a good stroke on the ball.

"Looking forward in the direction of the cup, the golden gutter may curve, following any break in the green and then extending all the way into the hole. If I'm having a really good day, I can even see which side of the hole the gutter empties into. Right near the end of the golden gutter, I visualize a shocking pink 1916-D Mercury dime. This could be just in front of the cup, in a downhill putt, or just behind the cup, if an uphill putt. I visualize the ball rolling right over this imaginary coin just before it drops in."

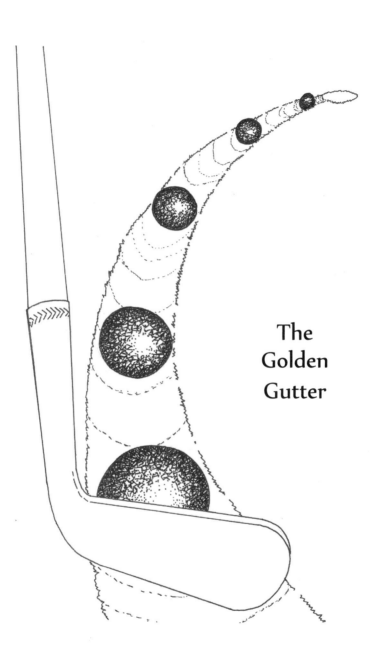

The
Golden
Gutter

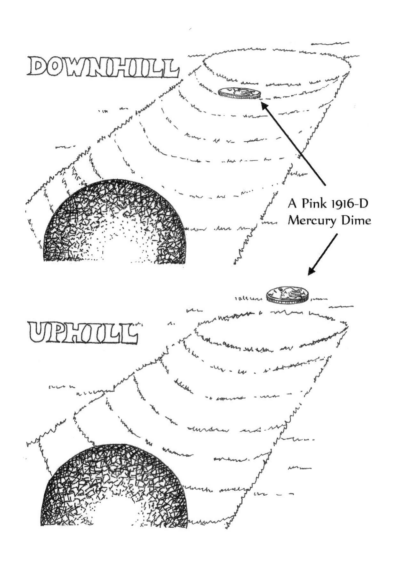

DOWNHILL

A Pink 1916-D
Mercury Dime

UPHILL

"I chose the 1916-D dime because it is so rare and artistically designed. I paint the dime shocking pink so it too presents itself vividly in my mind. In fact, I cannot *not* see it!

"As we discussed before, Right Thought, which encompasses visualization, also requires the use of Right Concentration, better known as sharp focus. They work together. Think of a manual camera. You can frame an image, but it also needs to be in sharp focus to be a good picture. Likewise, you've got to *create a visualized image in your mind's eye, then hold your focus on it*. If I do have any trouble obtaining the image or the focus, then I simply paint the colors of the gutter or the dime or both something a little more crazy, maybe candy apple red or surf green, hip colors I borrowed from 1950s and 60s America. Changing the color in my mind helps me start over with renewed images.

"If I'm using a putter, but I can't consistently see the gutter and the dime, then that particular putter is no good for me. I don't care how it's designed, who made it, or what it cost. It still could be a very good putter for someone else with a different set of visualization keys, but not for me. Said another way, if you cannot visualize and hold focus on your putts, buy any putter you wish, none will be effective. The physical putting tool alone makes no matter when you use the power of the Eightfold Path tools. Now there's more to it than that, but I think you get the idea for now."

As I try to absorb all that, I'm thinking, "Whoa! Buddha is sounding even more cosmic than before with all this jazz, but now let's see him sink this treacherous 15-foot putt." Buddha confronts his current challenge. I sense his concentration as he deeply visualizes his golden gutter curving along that nasty left-to-right break, falling away from a right-hander. He sees his putt channeling down that bending gutter then rolling directly over that shocking pink 1916-D Mercury dime at the front of the cup.

Only after he precisely sees these pictures is he ready. With bold confidence, he strokes it. The ball channels down the golden gutter, rolling, curving right, now slowing, still curving right, then over the pink Mercury dime and *in*. Bingo, a birdie two.

Holy smoke, this guy is now *four-under* par after only *five* holes. I'm thinking to heck with that $349 (plus tax) laser-beam endowed putter I just saw at my local pro shop last Saturday. Visualization and focus, indeed! Then I had an epiphany: In over 35 years I've spent about a million hours on the putting green, but have I actually been practicing all the *wrong* stuff?

Visualize or "see" the golden gutter and the pink mercury dime. Keep both in sharp focus as you stroke your putt.

BUDDHA'S CORNER
A Fifth Element of the Eightfold Path

ON RIGHT CONCENTRATION

As you try out putters at your local golf shop or warm-up putting green, remember that you must *practice*—there's that word again—Right Concentration. Just stroking putts, without having the mind images *together with* sharp focus won't help you on the course, especially when the pressure's on.

How much you practice is not as important as *what* you practice.

The putter that best facilitates your *visualization and sharp focus* of the putt you are about to stroke is the best putter for you.

Use any putter you wish, but as you master both visualization and razor-sharp focus, watch your putts start to drop.

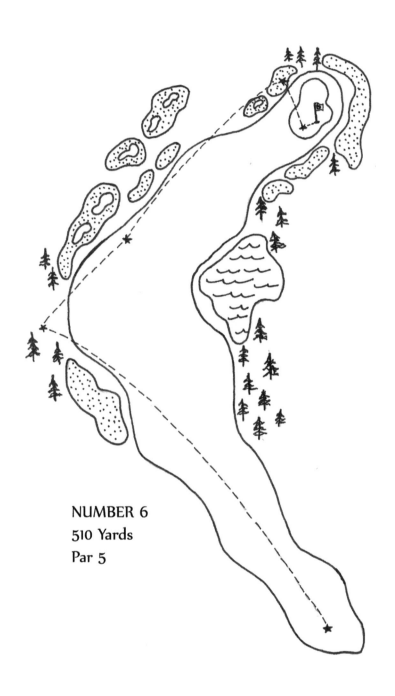

NUMBER 6
510 Yards
Par 5

NUMBER 6
510 Yards, Par 5

Caddy's View from the Tee:

Six large fairway bunkers (err... *"opportunities") are left starting at about 230 from the tee, and a pine forest and pond are to the right. The wind is right-to-left. The fairway slopes severely left-to-right, balls can easily roll into the water hazard. If all this weren't hard enough, you've got three huge bunkers to deal with all around this green.*

Space-age technology has long since come to golf. Titanium, graphite, boron, stainless steel, Kevlar, over-sized metal drivers, cavity-backed irons, forged heads, cast heads, computerized club-fitting, swing radar guns, two piece low-spin balls, three-piece high-spin balls, GPS satellite systems, laser rangefinder distance calculators, and more. (Note to all non-golfers: No, I'm not making any of this stuff up!)

As caddy, I'm standing at the tee thinking that what we need here is obvious: A monster long, 8-degree titanium driver with the maximum USGA-legal 460 cubic centimeters of club head volume, optimum moment of inertia, coupled to the latest low-torque boron-graphite composite shaft and all-leather pro wrap grip. We've just got to have the distance to clear the center fairway rough, and we don't want a blind shot or lay-up into the green. (Maybe with my expert analysis I can even earn a fat tip after the round. After all, I *am* Buddha's caddy, and I haven't done a thing to really help him so far today, but hey, this could be my big chance.) Trouble is, Buddha is carrying very traditional clubs. He doesn't have the hi-tech driver stick he needs here, in my humble caddy-opinion.

Solution? I can run out right now and purchase a new hi-tech driver for him. Better yet, I saw an illegal, monster 898cc titanium driver with internal spring-loaded plutonium shaft being sold out of the back of some guy's trunk at the parking lot when we came in this morning. Now, *there's* a war club that can get Buddha on this green in one, especially if I pick up a sleeve of those illegal, super-steroid injected helium golf balls to go with it!

I run this notion past Buddha. He looks at me sideways, "You can't be serious! This would violate Right Action, which requires honesty, fairness, compassion, love, and so many other things. You can't use crazy ideas to try to get ahead, get a raise, get a new (or additional) girlfriend, or improve your golf score. People who do dishonest things like this are lost—and they just become more lost as they continue to try to cheat their way to happiness. It turns into a hideous cycle of suffering. But don't hate them for their actions; offer them compassion because they are so very lost. After all, none of us are perfect. We all fight these emotional battles within ourselves."

After hearing all that, I realize it's no wonder Buddha wants his totally legal, non-state-of-the-art, driver at the tee. He hooks it left and long into the deep rough, almost 280 yards out. A tremendously powerful hit, but misdirected and in definite trouble. His second shot, in a terrible side hill lie, is a recovery shot just pitched out of the rough with an 8-iron and back into the fairway. His third is a 150-yard 6-iron out of another poor lie into yet more trouble, this time the sand bunker left. What's going on here?

Now the pressure shot: Lying three in a bunker, Buddha needs an up and down to save par. Finally some good news as the ball is sitting up nicely in the sand. Buddha's sand wedge pops him out to within four feet. Buddha discusses his "out" with, "I visualize a children's purple wading pool sitting on the green. When I'm pitching or chipping, I just try to softly bounce the ball into the wading pool, and let it roll the rest of the way.

"Of course, I also need to study the grain and break of the green and adjust the lob distance to the wading pool. I hold my arms steady and put a pendulum-type stroke on the ball; more like a putt than a swing. Also—very important—I need to once more concentrate on keeping my head down and steady, all the way through the short swing—no peeking."

Just "bounce" your pitch into the "wading pool" circle landing area.

"I even like to wait until I hear the ball bounce into the pool before I look up. This sounds quite easy, but it's not unless you've practiced it."

Buddha next reiterates that we must also continuously practice the Eightfold Path principles to eliminate our "bad shots" in life as well as golf. To illustrate the point, he explains, "If my swing path is wrong, the results will not be what I want. With that last errant shot, a hi-tech driver would have sent me *even further* into the deep rough. Ha! I didn't need a *better club*; I needed a *better swing*!" With this he laughs at himself, apparently another important Buddhist trait.

"I'm not going to look to my driver or to any other club in my bag to explain my problems. Even with a million-dollar golf club, legal or illegal, your ball direction result is a function of your swing path and club head direction.

"Of course, it's always far easier to look to the *external* forces like golf clubs, distractions, weather, or even an ex-spouse and blame *them* instead of recognizing our own shortcomings. But the *path you've followed*, either in your golf swing or life, is the ultimate factor at the moment of truth. You can whiff a driver or slam it 320 yards down the middle of the fairway. Either of those things can happen with the same club in your hands."

Okay, time for a quick review of some early basics: On this hole it's obvious to Buddha that he has a frustrated and upset caddy. This again highlights that the First Noble Truth, *Golf is Suffering*, is alive and well. According to Buddha, my mere desire for a new driver, legal or illegal, is in itself a basic cause of life's suffering. This desire creates "attachments," as discussed earlier, and encompasses Buddhist philosophy's Second Noble Truth: The attachments alone set up a relentless flow of golf suffering. Which leads us to the Third Noble Truth: Eliminate the attachments, and you will eliminate the suffering. And to eliminate the attachments, we go to the Fourth Noble Truth: We must practice the Eightfold Path.

As a postscript, my being tempted to buy Buddha an illegal driver (and golf ball to boot) is not in keeping with the tenets of Right Actions, an element of the Eightfold Path. In other words, cheating won't get you into the International Golfer's Hall of Fame.

Back to Buddha's golf game. Buddha takes out his 1920s low-tech, wood-shafted, blade putter and one putts his four-footer to save par. We're 4-under par after six.

BUDDHA'S CORNER
A Sixth Element of the Eightfold Path

ON RIGHT ACTIONS
Cheating won't get you into the
International Golfer's Hall of Fame.

ON GOLF EQUIPMENT AND YOUR SWING

Try this parallel: In terms of golf, while on your **golf swing's** journey, think more about the purity of your swing **"path"** and less about the specs of the club you're holding onto along the way. And while on your **life's** journey, think more about traveling along the **Eightfold Path** and less about the material objects you're holding onto along the way. Get it?

ON CHIPS AND PITCHES

Visualize a children's purple wading pool, and lob your pitches into it; use a pendulum-type swing and don't pressure yourself. Stay down, steady and through the ball. Listen for the ball to plop into the wading pool before looking up—and no peeking!

BUDDHA'S CORNER

SWING VISUALIZATIONS RECAP

Using a black felt tip marker, write down your swing thought keywords onto the sole plate (soul plate) of your driver and other woods. Buddha uses EDS, 8-I and THRU (Easy Down Swing, 8-iron and follow-THRU), but it's important to make up your own, personal swing thoughts. Every time you pull that club out, you'll be immediately and directly reminded of those swing thoughts! This works—give it a chance!

Visualize Buddha's "orange stake" well back and behind your right pocket (assuming you're a right-handed golfer) and gently hit the stake down into the ground as you begin your downswing (i.e., your first move down). This usually works best if you try to drive your left hand down onto the stake as you start down with your swing. If you are having trouble seeing the stake, keep changing its color in your mind until you can see it more vividly. In the downswing, don't try to hammer down too hard or swing too fast as those actions will cause your right shoulder to jet out— the kiss of death, resulting in the infamous "out-to-in" swing path and the dreaded slice, pull, or pull-slice.

When putting, see the pink 1916D Mercury dime lying just in front of the hole. See the color and the reflection of the dime in the sunlight. The shorter the putt, the more important this visualization exercise. If you are having trouble seeing the dime, change its color—and change its color on every green if necessary.

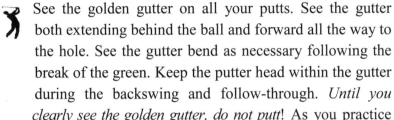

See the golden gutter on all your putts. See the gutter both extending behind the ball and forward all the way to the hole. See the gutter bend as necessary following the break of the green. Keep the putter head within the gutter during the backswing and follow-through. *Until you clearly see the golden gutter, do not putt*! As you practice this more, you will see it easily and quickly. Change the color of the gutter as necessary. After a while, you will never allow yourself to putt without first seeing the gutter. When you've reached that point with this all-important putting visualization, you've arrived!

On chips and even short pitches, see the purple children's wading pool on the landing area and put the ball into the pool, letting it roll the rest of the way to the pin. If you are having trouble seeing the pool, change the pool's color until you can see it vividly. Do not chip or pitch until you see the pool as your landing area. Keep your head still and down through the shot—don't look up until you actually hear the ball hit the pool. (Yeah, I know, easier said than done, but practice it and watch your short game drastically improve!)

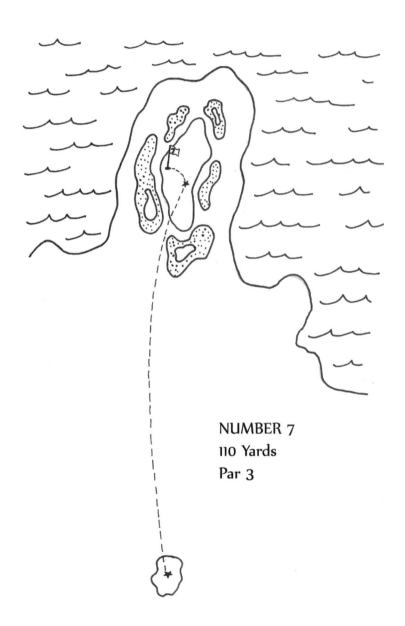

NUMBER 7
110 Yards
Par 3

NUMBER 7
110 Yards, Par 3

Caddy's View from the Tee:

This can be one tough challenge as the winds off the water can swirl and change from moment to moment. And if the winds weren't enough, there are bunkers everywhere to swallow up any stray shot. Short? You're in a bunker "opportunity." Long? There is virtually no space behind this green, so you'll be swimming. Right or left? You're in the sand or the water. And the green is well below the elevated tee. You never really know what you're up against here until after you've hit your tee shot.

Since Number 7 is all about changing winds, what does Buddhism have to say about both change and dealing with change? Plenty. For starters, Buddha claims, "Consider that everything is constantly changing, not just the wind here at the tee on Number 7. In fact, I'm not even the identical person I was when I left that last green just a moment ago, and you are not the same caddy that you were when we started our round this morning. That course out there and the wind are never the same from millisecond to millisecond. Even the grass in front of us is growing taller as we stand here admiring the beauty around us. There is no permanent Hole 7 or me or you or anything else. Every person or thing is making a *guest* appearance."

As if Mother Nature herself heard Buddha's words, the winds suddenly pick up drastically, now coming straight into us at a blistering 40 to 50 miles per hour. The flag at the pin is fully extended in the wind and pointing directly toward us, not a good sign. But Buddha couldn't care less. "I cannot control the wind, so I'm not going to worry about it. In fact, I can't control anything except myself in this moment, so I'm not going to worry about a thing. Staying in the present moment is Right Mindfulness."

He continues, "Right Knowledge is the culmination of the Eightfold Path, and it leads us to the awareness of change. Five elements: The things around you, your sensations, perception, mental state, and responses are always in flux. We are made up of these 'five aggregates' and nothing more. Once you realize that the perception of a fixed 'I' is an illusion and as such is just another attachment that you need to remove, you will be shooting aces, eagles, and birdies on your road to enlightenment."

But that sparks a Western world observation from me: "If Right Knowledge is the culmination of the Eightfold Path, why not just go straight to that and forget the other seven principles? I mean I want to take the fast lane on my road to enlightenment! Express, non-stop service at the drive-through, if you get my drift."

Buddha's comeback: "Because you need all of the other seven principles to get to Right Knowledge. In golf or life, you can't just skip holes, miss opportunities or challenges, or take convenient shortcuts and then call it a full round.

"It's sort of like playing this shot into the strong wind. There are no shortcuts. We have to do the right things and execute. I'll widen my stance for better stability, put the ball back in my stance, choke down on my club to keep the ball flight low, swing slow, and punch the ball with a shortened follow-through. The ball will come out a little hot, but low, and will run."

And with that, Buddha punches his ball dead into a near gale force wind with a 100-yard choked down 4-iron. Even in this hellacious weather, his swing stays smooth. Three bounces short of the green, his ball hits and rolls up onto the dance floor. He has a 6-foot putt remaining, left-to-right. He visualizes, focuses, and sinks it.

Another bird on the scorecard. And a whole lot of new wisdom for me to think about from what I just heard and saw. Changes? I don't think any golf hole will be the same for me ever again. And somehow the winds, trees, and waves make the course seem even more beautiful. We move to 5-under par after seven. Yeah, Buddha may seem cosmic at times, but I'm digging this guy, and, man, does he have "game!"

BUDDHA'S CORNER
A Seventh Element of the Eightfold Path

ON RIGHT MINDFULNESS

Stay in present moment reality as you play the course. Do not be distracted by your last bad shot; that is an attachment. Illusions, such as where your ball should have gone or could have gone mean nothing—since your ball is not there anyway.

Where your ball sits *in reality* is all that matters.

HITTING INTO THE WIND

Widen your stance for stability; put the ball back in your stance. Swing slow and low, sort of punching the ball. Keep your follow-through short and low. Watch club selection, you want your shot to stay low and roll.

And don't forget to practice at the range. You can't hit consistently spectacular shots without first studying the components of the perfect golf swing. You can't get to the top of the leader board in the U.S. Open without learning and practicing *all* the fundamentals. At the highest levels, pure great golf, just like Buddhist philosophy, has no true shortcuts."

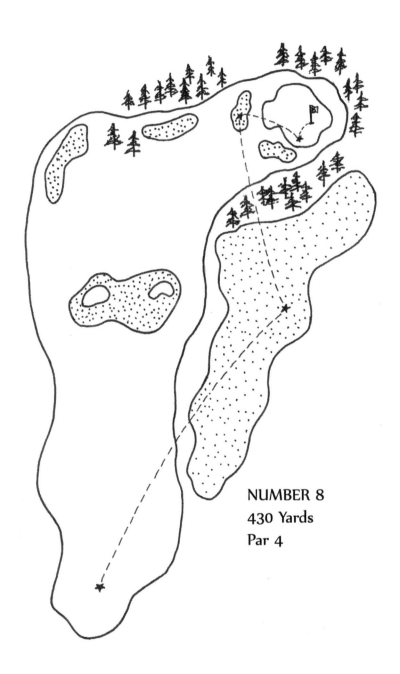

NUMBER 8
430 Yards
Par 4

NUMBER 8
430 Yards, Par 4

Caddy's View from the Tee:

Number 8 is a huge challenge, but a gorgeous one. The rough is big trouble right. It's about 280 out to the dogleg knee. The landing area of the fairway is very wide, but a huge bunker goes across the fairway at about 220 out. Too far left makes this par 4 play longer due to the dogleg right. The prevailing winds continue to push strongly to right. Pines surround the green, including the back— so don't be long on your all-important approach shot. Sand bunkers guard the front of the green. This green is large, but with severe breaks, back to front.

In his worst shot of the day, Buddha slices driver an incredible distance into the stiff wind. The left-to-right wind only magnifies the ball's sidespin. As we leave the tee box, we pass by a beautiful bed of dahlias, bending with the breezes. Buddha observes, "When I see flowers, I rejoice. What a glorious interaction of earth, wind and sky."

"Yeah, but what about that sliced drive you just hit deep into that huge right waste area?" I cautiously tease.

"Aw, forget it," he responds. "The greatest mistake is to be always afraid of making one. Instead of getting angry or frustrated with that less-than-beautiful shot, I'll accept the situation with calmness and focus on constructive efforts. I understand a 'bad' shot, so I can let it go. I'll stay within the present moment and use Right Mindfulness. By staying in the present reality, I'll correct my 'mistake' and move along on our journey. I saw Jack Nicklaus interviewed on TV, and he said that he honestly couldn't remember most of his lousy shots, but he vividly remembered all his iconic shots, of which there were many. That's perfect thinking coming from one of the greatest golfers of all time."

"In fact, nothing here is really 'bad.' I'm merely confronted with some new exciting challenges in my next shot. You too need to see it that way. Your journey has 'challenges,' not 'errors.' Change the negative words you use to positive words, and your brain will eventually get the message. Then your thinking will change the same way, from negative to positive. It's pretty cool how this works—and very powerful."

Buddha now thoughtfully considers his remedies. This rough is hardpan, ugly-type ground cover stuff. I'm skeptical about his ability to recover from this one, and I warn him, "I doubt that you can get out in one; this hole is spelling disaster. You might easily ruin your entire round." (You guessed it. I was wrong yet again.)

Buddha replies, "The only cure for doubt is Right Mindfulness, not backing off or running away from the moment of challenge, but by staying in it instead. Once you stay in the situation, keeping your thoughts positive, you can get through it and let go of it. I'm not expecting to get out of this easily or even make the green from here. In fact, I can't even *see* the green from here! I'm not expecting a darn thing. But my lack of attachment—*expecting nothing*—will allow me to put a nice swing path on the ball. Right Mindfulness will keep me in the present moment—and I will meet this opportunity successfully."

Oh brother! All I know is that he's on hardpan with a blind shot to the green—his toughest shot of the day so far. Tempting as it may be, I think I had better hold my tongue, per one of Buddha's earlier lessons this morning concerning Right Speech.

Whack! A 160-yard clean 6-iron fades slightly right, typical for a hardpan lie. He flies the narrow fairway and rolls all the way into the left greenside bunker. Okay, it's another sand shot and no picnic, but from where he was it could have been way worse. I'm impressed.

Buddha splashes long out of the sand "opportunity" and then drops a really tough seven-foot, left-to-right, downhill putt for par. Whew. A major disaster was averted.

We're hanging in there, still admirably at 5-under par after eight holes.

BUDDHA'S CORNER
Eighth Element of the Eightfold Path

ON RIGHT KNOWLEDGE

If Right Knowledge is the culmination of the Eightfold Path, why not just go straight to the top by going into deep meditation and forget the earlier seven principles? Buddha teaches, **"Because you need all of the other seven principles to get to Right Knowledge—there are no short-cuts."**

ON USING POSITIVE WORDS INSIDE YOUR GOLF GAME

Rather than mentally labeling something as "trouble" or "bad," just think "opportunities" or "challenges."

Change your *words* from negative to positive and you'll change your *thinking* from negative to positive. Your mind will then instruct your muscles to change your *actions* from negative to positive. *Then* watch your golf scores drop! Believe it.

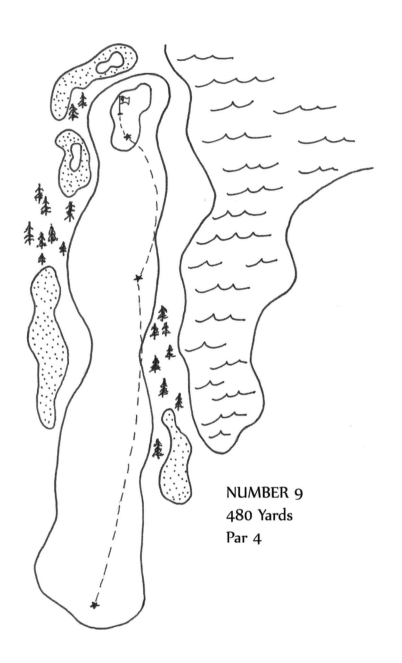

NUMBER 9
480 Yards
Par 4

NUMBER 9
480 Yards, Par 4

Caddy's View from the Tee:

If Number 8 started off as a bad dream, 9 could potentially become a nightmare. A very long par 4 with bunkers and trees left. If you're going to draw the ball for the much needed greater distance, you better do it carefully. The fairway slopes downhill left-to-right toward the water hazard, so your shot into the green will be from a tough side-hill lie with your ball angling away from you, begging a slice. The wind is again in play, blowing across right-to-left off the water. If you're on in two, you're doing great on this hole.

After that miraculous save for par at Number 8, you would think Buddha would want to cautiously back off here. No way. There is very little "lay-up" in Buddha. Life is a continuous challenge that he does not fear—but, on the other hand, he isn't reckless or irresponsible either.

There's really no choice but driver off the tee, given the hole layout. Buddha lets it rip with a booming 270-yard draw. He starts it right and brings it in slightly to rest just on the right edge of the fairway. He has just hit one of his best shots of the day on probably the toughest hole on the course. We start our jubilant walk down the ninth fairway.

From a perfect lie, Buddha hits his second shot on Number 9, a nice 5-wood draw of about 210 yards. It's a wonderful shot, flying high and landing soft, right on target. He's got a 7-foot uphill, front-to-back putt for birdie. After a longer-than-usual putt visualization (this time I could almost feel him seeing his "golden gutter") and his usual period of focused concentration, he sinks it. Hey, chalk up another birdie for Right Thought and Right Concentration.

After witnessing his great drive and beautiful approach shot, I feel compelled to ask Buddha more about the perfect golf swing. He slowly nods, smiles and replies, "There are a million angles in a golf swing; just pick up a book on golf fundamentals—it's all so mechanically intricate. But, when the clubface actually contacts the ball, in that one moment of truth, all is decided. How you get to the ball doesn't actually matter. The swing path journey can be different for every golfer, but as long you maintain certain fundamentals, the results can be very worthwhile and rewarding.

"But that single moment of ball contact must be pure for great results. In essence, I just swing, using the correct path, and the ball happens to be there, in the way. Just like in life, this all takes diligent practice. But what you practice makes all the difference. Working hard is always seen as a virtue, and yes, you do need to work hard at practice—but you must practice the right things—including how you think, not just how you swing."

Okay, I get that, theoretically anyway. But, I'm not so sure I can actually do everything he's been talking about on the golf course, as good as it all sounds. In one part of my gut, I still feel like I need countless hours at the driving range with my clubs, hitting balls out endlessly, refining my swing mechanics. But in another part of my gut, I feel like maybe I'm practicing much of the wrong stuff in light of Buddha's positive mental perspective on the game.

As I reflect on everything he's said today, I wonder if I am learning and moving forward or getting confused and going backward? Buddha studies me a moment and then says, "No pain, no gain. Isn't that one of your pop culture's expressions? This applies to new thinking as well as to just gym workouts, you know. Growing pains in your mind are a very good thing."

We're now officially at the turn, and our golf journey is half-over. We wander over to the small on-course refreshment shop. A gorgeous, suntanned blond gal with a beautiful smile is behind the counter—what else would you expect at a fabulous California course? Chalk another one up for Right Action. Buddha shows no lust for the attractive woman. (I'm sorry to say that his caddy may be a bit weaker in this department.)

Buddha takes in a drink from the public water fountain. He just can't get excited about "highbrow drinking water encapsulated in plastic bottles," as he calls it. He mumbles something about landfills and the environment. He orders: "Hot dog, please—hold the meat." (I've learned since that Buddhists do not have to be vegetarians—that is a common misconception.)

All morning long I have been awkwardly scribbling notes while simultaneously fumbling with Buddha's golf bag up the fairways. As I read over my notes here at the turn, my mind starts swirling like the wind. I ponder how amazing it is that Buddha shifts so effortlessly in his thinking back and forth between Buddhist philosophy and golf. I must admit that it all *sounds* right as he applies the Eightfold Path principles to each shot on each hole. And, bottom line, I certainly can't argue with his current score. With my adrenaline flowing, I'll force down a beverage and a bag of chips while I review and double-check the scorecard.

I see an astonishingly good round so far. Buddha's got six birdies and three pars across the front, yielding a 6-under par 30. He hit some superb iron and sand shots and had a run of sweet one-putts. And he did all this on a challenging course in a swirling, changing, unpredictable wind. What was even more impressive was that when he did make an occasional miscue, he recovered without blowing his cool or his score. More than anything, I think he demonstrated a certain *positive attitude* and *wisdom* as he played the front nine. If he keeps this up, we are closing in on the Enlightenment Golf & Country Club course record of 62. Pretty darn amazing!

ENLIGHTENMENT GOLF & COUNTRY CLUB

HOLE	1	2	3	4	5	6	7	8	9	OUT	10	11	12	13	14	15	16	17	18	IN	TO-TAL
BLUE	406	522	404	337	190	510	110	430	480	3389	441	383	212	403	580	457	444	155	555	3630	7019
WHITE	380	490	370	327	190	470	110	400	440	3177	430	370	200	375	510	390	430	165	490	3360	6527
HDCP	6	4	10	8	16	2	18	12	14		5	7	15	9	3	11	13	17	1		
BUD-DHA	3	4	4	3	2	5	2	4	3	30											
PAR	4	5	4	4	3	5	3	4	4	36	4	4	3	4	5	4	4	3	5	36	72
RED	300	420	320	310	170	410	100	335	365	2730	345	340	170	310	410	300	351	135	388	2749	5479

BUDDHA'S CORNER
ON THE PERFECT GOLF SWING

Study the fundamentals. Learn and feel confident that you are on the right swing "path." Then swing on this path, and let the ball just happen to be there. Starting with your take-away, swing slowly, naturally, and all the way through—what's your big hurry anyway? This sounds easy, but it actually takes diligent practice.

> Golf practice includes mental
> as well as physical activities.

> "No pain, no gain" applies to
> the mind as well as the body.

Working hard is always seen as a virtue, especially in the Western world, and you *do* need to work hard at practice—but you also must practice the *right* things, including your new *thinking*.

One thing is for sure: I don't want this round to end. How much more can I learn from Buddha with another nine holes yet to play? To be honest, I'm not really sure what to expect next.

Out to Number 10.

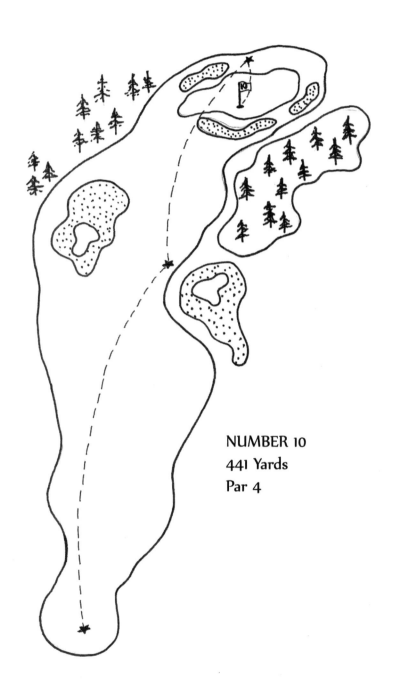

NUMBER 10
441 Yards
Par 4

NUMBER 10
441 Yards, Par 4

Caddy's View from the Tee:

There's still a lot of real estate ahead of us on our back nine journey: Number 10 is another fairly long par 4 with a deep grove of pines right, a huge fairway bunker out about 250 from the tee, and another large bunker in the landing area to the right. The fairway slopes severely left-to-right, toward the woods. Going right is tricky as the ball will tend to roll right and into the bunker or rough.

After his pre-shot routine, Buddha puts his 3-wood drive into orbit; it's a controlled fade of about 260 yards. The fade spin was imparted with a slight out-to-in swing path and open clubface, making the ball land softly and curtailing its roll. The ball comes to rest on the right side of the fairway but just short of the dreaded pine forest and rough. A near-perfect opening shot on the back nine.

Buddha takes his next shot from a square stance (his right foot even with his left foot), and this time hits a fairly straight 3-iron, bouncing twice then stopping on the apron to the back left, just off the green. He's got a 16-foot chip to the cup. He opens up his stance slightly for this one and chips it dead straight on line. Buddha explains, "On the chip-and-run shots like this, I always visualize where I want to land the ball. Just like before, I 'see' a children's purple wading pool of about three-foot diameter. I try to softly lob the ball into that pool." He chips it; the ball falls softly into the imaginary pool, then runs and drops into the cup. Birdie 3.

I saw Buddha use no less than three slightly different techniques on this hole. His drive was a gorgeous high fade brought about by an "out-to-in" swing and slightly open clubface. His approach shot was a beautiful 3-iron from a square stance and perfect release of his hands. And his chip for birdie was practically dead straight with an open stance while using virtually no hand action at all. And even though all three set-ups, swings, and hand actions were somewhat different, every shot worked. This proves another of Buddha's points: We can get from point A to point B around a golf course in many different ways.

"Go to a driving range and observe," Buddha suggests. "You will see a hundred poor souls swinging a club about a thousand different ways to try to get to that pathetic little 1.62-ounce golf ball. Most people don't even have a ball direction in mind or a target—they just keep swinging aimlessly—figuratively and literally. Sadly, they may go through their whole lives the same way with no consistent application; no practicing of the fundamentals; just chasing after attachments; and lots of suffering.

"There are only *three* fundamental swing paths into the golf ball, out-to-in, in-to-out, and square. But to make any of these three swing paths work for you, a number of basic principles have to be followed within the swing. And they must be followed consistently. That comes only through practice.

"It's like Buddhism. You see, we have three broad variations or schools (or 'vehicles' or 'yanas') of Buddhist philosophy: Theravada, Mahayana, and Vajrayana. If you consistently practice the fundamentals of any one of them, you can get to the ultimate flagstick, Nirvana or enlightenment. You might want to learn more about all three schools, or you could just naturally be drawn to one. In the Western world, Mahayana is the most practiced.

"But for now, don't sweat it. Just recognize that like hitting a golf ball with draw, fade or square path, the three Buddhist schools are sort of the draw, fade and square of the Buddhist philosophy. Of course, I'm oversimplifying things here. There are many more details and complexities to Buddhism, but I think you get the general idea. You can get from A to B in different ways."

But back to golf. After Buddha's birdie, we're now 7-under par through 10 holes. Man, this round may go from the remarkable to the miraculous, if he keeps *this* up.

Since every golf instructor talks about grip, I figure I had better ask Buddha about it while I've got the chance. He just smiles, thinks for a moment, then replies, "There's not much I can add to what's been already been written about it over the decades, but your grip is critical because it is the only contact you ultimately have with the ball. Since there are about a million golf book chapters on the topic, there's little need to go into great depth on it again here, but I will say that in line with Buddhist thinking, it is best to keep this grip stuff simple.

"There are three grip styles normally preached: overlapping, interlocking, or baseball. Just choose the grip that feels most natural to you, and don't worry about what others do or think. Golf is hard enough without forcing yourself into what someone else thinks you are supposed to do! I used a baseball grip for years, and then later switched to overlapping. There is no one best grip style for everyone—or every pro on earth would be using it.

"Buddhist thinking never involves brute force. Likewise, don't squeeze the life out of your club shafts, something golfers too commonly do. Gentle pressure is all you need so you can turn the club over at impact. If you are getting holes in your golf glove or developing calluses, your grip is too tight—probably, *way* too tight. Firm wrists result in your hands acting more like a ping-pong paddle as you come into the ball and will usually give you a ball direction of a push or fade because your club head face will be open at impact. This is also known as a form of 'blocking.' Firm wrists are excellent for consistent putting or chipping, but not for a full swing, as you lose all leverage of your golf club tool. Can you imagine using a screwdriver or hammer with stiff wrists?

"Next, assuming you're a right-handed golfer, move your grip right (or 'stronger') to generate a more closed clubface at impact for a draw or hook, and move your grip left (or more on top of the shaft or 'weaker') to generate a neutral or more open clubface, generating a fade. At address, most amateurs should see two or almost three knuckles of their left hand, which would result in a somewhat strong grip, promoting a draw (or right-to-left secondary ball direction), theoretically anyway. Depending on the many other components of your swing, try different grip positions on the practice range, and watch your ball direction carefully. Keep moving your hands to the right until the ball is consistently drawing right-to-left in its secondary direction.

"'But Houston, we have a problem' in that the directions I just gave assume that as you alter your grip position on the shaft, everything else in your swing will stay the same. This is rarely the case among amateur players. In other words, it is *very hard* to get consistent results just by rotating your grip position. For example, if you rotate your grip to the right to try to get more right-to-left action on the ball, chances are that you will also now, consciously or unconsciously, swing more from the outside or 'over the top' to 'help' move the ball left. So, now your ball may well start left (a pull), then go more left due to your strong grip. The result is the dreaded 'pull-hook.' Not good. In contrast, if you rotate your hands stronger (to the right) on the shaft, you might develop a tendency to *not* rotate your wrists through the ball, resulting in blocking out at impact and the ball slicing right anyway. Okay, so what's the bottom line here? Simply this: Control of the secondary direction of your ball via your grip (producing fades and draws at will) takes diligent, long-term practice. Stay realistic! Expectations are an *attachment*, and attachments lead to suffering, remember?

"I'm totally amazed at the slick, worn out grips I see in use on the golf course. As any self-respecting Buddhist handyman will tell you that without control of your tools you have nothing. Guys and gals might spend well over $1,000 on fourteen clubs and then, for $100 or so, they won't replace their worn grips. Crazy, man!

"Oh, and one final thing: Before you chuck those worn grips into the trash bucket, take a close look at exactly where your grips show the most wear, club by club (and especially your driver and 3-wood). This will tell you a great deal about your grip pressure."

BUDDHA'S CORNER

GET A GRIP ON THINGS!

- Forget about what others do and choose a natural, comfortable grip style for *you*. There are three common grips: interlocking, overlapping or baseball.

- Don't strangle the holy life out of your poor, innocent clubs. Any wear-through on your golf glove is a telltale sign of way too much grip pressure.

- Experiment with different grip positions on the practice range, but don't expect miracle control of the ball without diligent, long-term practice.

- As you experiment and alter grip positions, put your usual swing on the ball in all other ways. (Warning: this is much easier said than done).

- Change your slick grips—today! Using worn grips on your tools makes a hard game just that much harder.

- Check the wear-points on each old grip; this can help you recognize and better understand any over-firm grip pressure; especially check your driver and 3-wood.

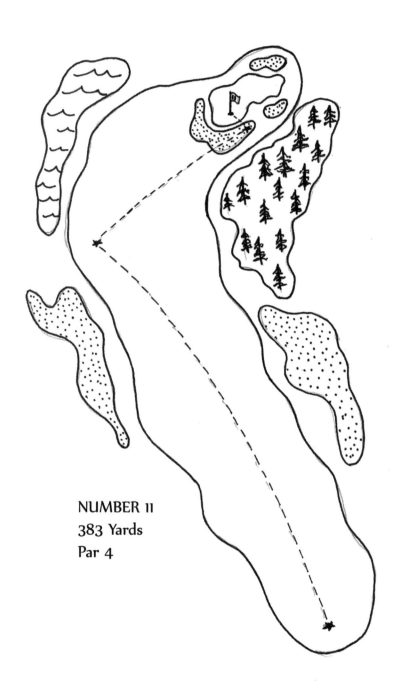

NUMBER 11
383 Yards
Par 4

NUMBER 11
383 Yards, Par 4

Caddy's View from the Tee:

Dogleg right. Hey, it's about time we get a par 4 at under 400 yards! And we're going to have the prevailing wind behind us to boot. But not so fast: We've got water left and deep woods right. Two giant waste area bunkers (opportunities!) line both sides of the fairway; the right side looks particularly menacing. We've got a wide fairway and the dogleg turns right at about 280 yards out from the tee. The narrow green severely slopes back to front so we don't want to go long on the critical approach shot, leaving a downhill putt. Three hungry-looking giant sand bunkers practically surround the green.

"5-wood, please," says the man in the orange robe. He sends a high right-to-left draw riding along the tail wind to about 240 yards. He lands just at the left edge of the fairway with a better-than-most chance to the green.

Buddha sizes up his next shot. He's got about 140 to the pin with the wind behind him. Going at the front pin placement, he goes with an easy 8-iron and loses it ever so slightly to the right catching the right-front bunker. "No big deal. Ha! I've got *plenty* of sand opportunity experience," he laughs at himself.

As we walk to his ball in the sand, we see a small anthill and a grasshopper, both in the trap. Buddha uses the occasion to recount an ancient story, "The ants are busy building their home in the sand for next winter and are also hard at work storing food. The grasshopper leisurely sits by and laughs at the ants, so preoccupied with their labors. When winter comes, the grasshopper will perish—he was irresponsible and did not take care of his future needs. The ants will survive the winter quite happily in the sand bunker." Using artistic license Buddha continues, "The sand bunker is seen as 'trouble' to a golfer but it is also providing a home and refuge for the ants. As for the grasshopper, the sand bunker is truly a trap that, *due only to his attitude,* will eventually cost him his life. So the moral is that it's all about *perspective* in life, on or off the golf course."

As Buddha enters his sand opportunity, he sees that the ball sits in an unfortunate position, like a fried egg in the center of the small depression it made upon landing in the sand. Seeing this lousy lie, I ask, "Hmm…what do you expect to do with *this*?"

"I don't expect a thing. I will just do my best to meet the challenge," he replies, then smiles and softly sweeps the ball out with his 56-degree sand wedge. It's a textbook sand shot with an out-to-in swing path. The ball pops out, slightly releases, and rolls uphill straight to the front edge of the cup, then ever so very slowly rolls and rolls yet another half-revolution and then drops in! Another bird!

Buddha explains, "As we saw before, expectations are just another form of want or desire, or in other words, just another type of 'attachment.' Attachments lead to suffering, so get rid of them. No expectations, no attachments. No attachments, no suffering. Bang-bang. Get it? Diligently practice the principles of the Eightfold Path, and eliminate your attachments. After all, it wasn't a magic trick that sank that last sand opportunity shot now was it?" He's right.

We're cookin' at 8-under through 11. I'm feverishly taking notes again as we walk.

BUDDHA'S CORNER
ON ATTACHMENT AND PAR 3s

I know I've said it before, but this one is worth repeating: Expectations are attachments, so *get rid of them.* If you expect a hole-in-one at every par 3, you are in for a lot of suffering. Take care of the important things both on the course and in life— remember the ants and the grasshopper.

BUDDHA'S CORNER

VOCABULARY, BALL DIRECTION, EXPECTATIONS

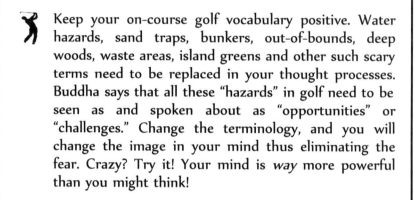 Keep your on-course golf vocabulary positive. Water hazards, sand traps, bunkers, out-of-bounds, deep woods, waste areas, island greens and other such scary terms need to be replaced in your thought processes. Buddha says that all these "hazards" in golf need to be seen as and spoken about as "opportunities" or "challenges." Change the terminology, and you will change the image in your mind thus eliminating the fear. Crazy? Try it! Your mind is *way* more powerful than you might think!

Buddha says that there are only three paths possible in a golf swing, so don't overly complicate things. Your ball's starting or ***primary direction*** will be dictated by your swing path and nothing else. If you are a right-handed golfer, you are normally swinging either:

Out-to-in (ball starts left)

In-to-out (ball starts right)

Square (ball starts dead straight; very rare)

Check your divot or tee direction at the practice tee for a clue to your starting or "primary" ball direction.

Assuming you're a right-handed golfer, your clubface (open, square or closed), will dictate the **secondary direction** of your ball:

Open face - ball moves right and bounces right as it hits; i.e., fade or slice.

Closed face - ball moves left and bounces left as it hits; i.e., draw or hook.

Square face - ball stays dead straight; very rare.

As your ball comes down, hits the ground and rolls, *keep your eye on it*—many amateurs don't! What is the ball telling you, and are you *listening?* You can, of course, change the clubface position at impact by moving your hands right or left within your grip—but remember that small changes can make a big difference. Lots of experimentation and practice will be necessary to permanently alter your grip.

 Buddha's advice about expectations: Keep them realistic. Golf is an extremely challenging game. Yes, you should expect improvement over time using Buddha's techniques, but don't expect to shave ten strokes off your handicap by next Saturday!

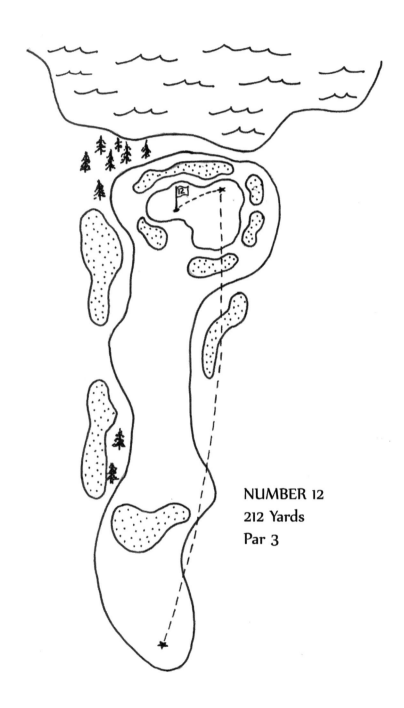

NUMBER 12
212 Yards
Par 3

NUMBER 12
212 Yards, Par 3

Caddy's View from the Tee:

There are really only two good strategies:

Either hit a soft shot and try to land it on the front of the green, or try to sneak the ball on by rolling it up the front of the green between the two huge front sand bunkers.

Either plan is far from easy to pull off. Most of the time a well-hit tee shot will be rolling off the back of this green and into the large bunker behind it. Anything long could find the pines or the water. The wind is in our faces at about 15 miles per hour.

We've finally caught up to a foursome that was way ahead of us most of the day. Three of them got into trouble here at 12 (sand, water, and pines). I get impatient and want the foursome to either putt out or wave us up—*now.* I yell ahead to them to get moving or let us play through. Buddha tells me to quiet down and relax. (It seems that every time I try to give advice or look out for my player, as a good caddy should, I come up in error. No exception this time either.)

Buddha pulls me out of earshot of the others and instructs, "The slow or stopped play on the hole is no reason to become impatient. Learn to welcome the stop signs in life. Use this time to breath deeply, enjoy the environment, and appreciate our journey around the course. We are at a magnificent spot, so getting slowed down actually lengthens our experience here—and what's the problem with *that?* There isn't one. So, cool it and just enjoy the delay.

"In fact, while we're on the subject, the huge majority of golfers *really need to slow down* anyway—they talk too fast, think too fast, walk too fast, drive cars too fast, eat too fast, lace their shoes too fast, and swing at a golf ball *way* too fast. As for the foursome in front of us, they have a right to play here too, so let them enjoy their moments just as we are enjoying ours. I don't feel it necessary that they wave us up or let us play through."

As his caddy, I've noticed something else. Buddha focuses on one thing at a time. He's always in the "present moment" or in Right Mindfulness, as he calls it. Right now he's totally—and I mean *totally*—focused on his upcoming challenging tee shot here at 12. After a few moments of waiting (which he spent calmly listening to the birds singing in the majestic pine trees), we're ready to go on.

Buddha goes through his pre-shot routine, visualizes, holds focus and smacks his 3-iron with a slight draw. Hitting the apron just to the left of the right front bunker, his ball rolls onto the front edge of the green then rolls about 20 feet past the cup.

Buddha explains, "My goal is to stay calm, relaxed, and mindful in the moment, no matter what the challenge. To accomplish that, I use a combination of the Eightfold Path principles of Right Thought, Right Concentration and Right Mindfulness or 'Zen,' and I have total confidence in my 3-iron. Then I just let go and swing. Once again, the ball just happens to be there."

Wait a second—I've heard that cosmic word "Zen" before— but did I also hear him say *"total confidence in a 3-iron?"* This Zen thing must be mighty powerful stuff indeed. Buddha just proved it with his excellent 3-iron draw.

Seeing the quizzical look on my face, Buddha explains, "Zen is an exotic Eastern word meaning 'mind,' or concentration in the present moment with focus, this all in the form of very deep meditation. Zen Masters are expert teachers. And those practicing with a Zen Master will experience the true nature of reality which cannot be expressed with words. Zen takes you into a new, clear awareness. But you need to use Zen not just in mediation sessions, but in your daily life as well, including out here on the golf course—maybe *especially* when you're holding a 3-iron in your hands. You can turn any golf shot or putt into an artistic and spiritual experience through practicing Zen." I think to myself, okay, fine…so let's see this mystical Zen work again, this time on the green for a pressure putt.

Buddha faces a 20-foot right-to-left downhill putt on a very firm green. I sense he's using his golden gutter and Mercury dime putting visualizations combined with sharp focus yet again. After some deep breathing he strokes it, never looks up, and sinks it. This is possibly his best putt of the round so far, and that's saying something.

A bit overwhelmed, I press him, "So through Zen practice, and using *that* level of awareness and confidence with every club, anything is possible?"

Buddha replies with his usual serene smile, "*Now* you're getting it. Yes, in fact, anything *is* possible."

We're 9-under through 12.

BUDDHA'S CORNER

You can experience Zen not only in deep meditation with a Zen Master but also on the golf course. Zen practice will turn your every golf shot into an artistic and spiritual experience. At the highest levels of Zen practice, you will have total confidence in every club in your bag, including that pesky 3-iron!

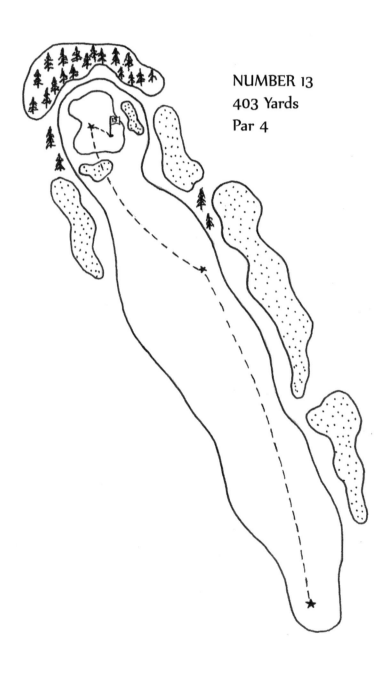

NUMBER 13
403 Yards
Par 4

NUMBER 13
403 Yards, Par 4

Caddy's View from the Tee:

We need control here. We have bunker waste areas all the way down the right side and severely sloping hill to the left side. Two small bunkers guard the green and a dense pine forest is behind the green. Not a tough hole if we stay out of trouble. Got to be careful not to hit the approach shot too far and over the green. The pin is cut in the front, right. Adding to our adventure, the green slopes severely back to front.

Lee Trevino brought two huge things to golf: a world famous controlled fade (using an out-to-in swing path) and a superb sense of humor. As to the latter, Buddha says that when you love life and approach it with humor, life loves you back. He says this is why the monks in the monasteries are always joking around. "Hey, if you're going to play golf, he says, "you had *better* develop a *great* sense of humor—especially when it comes to laughing at yourself. Otherwise you're in for a whole lot of frustration every time you take out your clubs. And frustration, yet another attachment, will take you on a non-stop flight direct to, you guessed it, more suffering."

And speaking of Trevino, after a fine 270-yard drive, Buddha goes to a Trevino-style fade for his 130-yard approach 8-iron. He leaves a 10-foot downhill putt to the left of the pin and observes, "Lee could have gotten it in closer to the pin, but I'm okay with it."

He strokes the putt, hitting it square with obvious authority and banging the ball smack into the back of the cup. No doubt about this one.

"You know that was a challenging downhill putt, but a golf course is a great environment to see Buddhist philosophy in action. As you can see, through my positive thoughts I've been able to meet most of my challenges here today. As I become more 'at one' with the beautiful environment of a golf course, it facilitates my mental processes."

Indeed. We've now had *five* birdies in a row and are 10-under through 13. Rock on, Buddha!

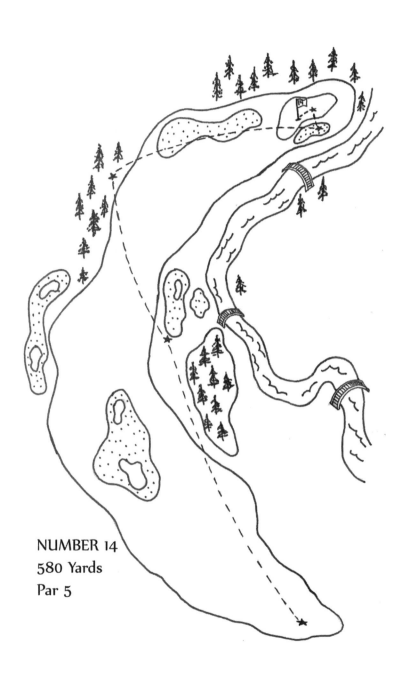

NUMBER 14
580 Yards
Par 5

NUMBER 14
580 Yards, Par 5

Arnold Palmer is by any and all accounts, a living legend. And as great a golfer that he was and is, he is remembered for so much more. A man of rock solid integrity and generosity—just his work with the hospital for children in Orlando alone is a testimonial to his compassion and principles. Buddha tells me that he has a great respect for people who live such exemplary lives. "Golf is minor," he says, "being a living legend for all the right reasons is major."

The wind has started to swirl. Buddha goes right with a fade drive of about 250 yards that reaches the heavy rough. From here, he selects a 5-wood out. He mis-hits it left across the fairway, and it rolls into the left rough about 160 yards from the pin. He goes with a 6-iron. The wind swirls strongly again, then just when he makes contact with his third shot, the wind suddenly dies out. As a result, his shot carries dead straight into the right-front greenside bunker. He hits out of the bunker with his 56-degree wedge and uncharacteristically two putts from 15 feet. Hmm...he's looking mortal again.

While we're on the topic of heavy rough, Buddha says that to get out of it, you need to accelerate through the ball, maintain the face square, and visualize the spot where you want to ball to land.

Stay down and through the shot with hands strong. Don't let the heavy rough alter your club's face angle into the ball. Of course, as he's said before, the rough is always an adventure or "opportunity," so don't let your expectations (attachments) get out of control. Just stay positive and put a good swing on the ball.

Tough as Number 14 is, I had expected Buddha to score better, much better, on this hole. Buddha tells me, "We talked about this before. There should be no expectations. Your renewed expectations of me led again to more suffering for yourself. I'm the one who hit the ball, and I'm not suffering because I had no expectations. On the other hand, you *are* suffering because you did. It's really that simple. Our serenity does not depend upon our *situations*, but rather on our *expectations*. You are having an adverse reaction to the lack of fulfilling an expectation you had of me."

He continues, "I cannot expect anything, and I cannot control the earth, the sky and the wind. Neither can you, so why are you trying? There are limitations in the physical world that you simply must accept. Let the earth, sky, stars and winds do as they wish."

As his well-intended caddy, I counter with a rant, "But you had a spectacular round going. That dang wind came up out of nowhere and blew your tee shot way right, then the wind died just as you hit your 6-iron third, and that put you into the greenside bunker. Not fair at all! Are you kidding me? That wind was absolutely nuts and may have even ruined your entire, brilliant round. Hey, do we even have to count this crummy hole? This is *bull*. Okay, at the *very least*, how about a couple of Mulligans? Without that unpredictable wind, you could have played this hole much, much better, I just *know* it."

"I'm afraid right now you *know* little," Buddha replies. "Your anger and frustration are both attachments that will only cause you even more suffering, now and later. If you think you want to *change* things, start with ever-improving yourself."

I retort, "Look, I'm trying to get it, I really am, but at times you sound so esoteric—*like the sound of one hand clapping.*"

With that, just as any good caddy should, I walk over to replace the pin to the cup after Buddha holes out. Disgusted, I mutter yet a few more four-letter words about the lousy weather that caused him the bogey. Just as I go to replace the pin into the cup, yet another blast of wind mysteriously swirls up out of nowhere, and the flag slaps me squarely across the face. Buddha smiles, turns to me and says, "*That*, my dear caddy, is the sound of one hand clapping!"

Unfortunately, we have bogied Number 14 and have backed off to 9-under par.

BUDDHA'S CORNER

At the Pebble Beach Crosby Pro-Am in 1967, Arnold Palmer trailed Jack Nicklaus by one stroke in the final round. On this particular Hole 14, Palmer's approach shot struck a tree and bounced out of bounds. He hit another shot, and struck the *same tree* again! He wound up taking a 9 on the hole and falling out of contention. That night a storm hit the Pebble Beach area, and strong winds ripped "Palmer's tree" right out of the ground!

Buddha says that we should never-underestimate the powers omnipresent on earth—nor, apparently, the powers of the King of Golf, Arnold Palmer.

"—like the sound of one hand clapping."

BUDDHA'S CORNER

PHILOSOPHICAL RECAP

Buddha says that we all need to slow down. Drive your car to the course slower. Eat slower. Walk slower. Talk slower. Drive the golf cart slower. Swing your clubs slower. Think slower. Write down your scores slower. Basically, *do everything slower* and watch your golf scores drop.

As a corollary to the above, don't get impatient on the course. For example, stop pressing that foursome in front of you. Why are *you* allowing *them* to wreck your golf game?

Getting mad at things you can't control won't help your game. Such action becomes misdirected and wasted energy forever lost to you.

Buddha claims that almost anything is possible if you see it in your mind and use Zen.

Buddha says not to fight either yourself or the course. Instead, be *at one* with the golf course, your round, the birds, the flowers, the trees, and your golf game. After all, a "bad" day golfing beats a lot of other things you could have been doing instead!

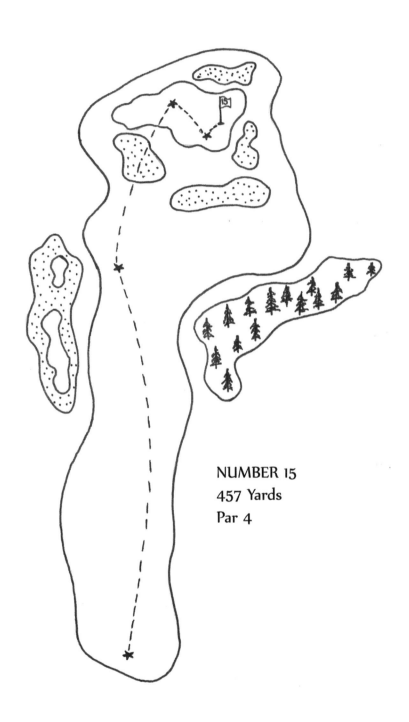

NUMBER 15
457 Yards
Par 4

NUMBER 15
457 Yards, Par 4

Caddy's View from the Tee:

Okay, okay, I need to compose myself after Buddha's bogey disaster at 14. Here at 15, the fairway is quite narrow in spots, and we have five bunkers and another forest in play. We can get home in two, and with an aggressive putt we can make up for the prior bogey.

The pesky wind has suddenly calmed. I offer my caddy advice, "C'mon Buddha, blast a huge driver off the tee, then take a wedge into the green for an aggressive one putt. We can make up for the bogey on that last hole here and now." (Yeah, I'm wrong yet again.)

Buddha instead chooses an easy 3-wood off the tee. He says not to get greedy and points out that it's wise here to give up some distance for accuracy in facing this narrow fairway. Characteristically he lays another velvet smooth swing on the ball. I notice that his follow-throughs are always so high and effortless—not easy for a stout guy weighing in at over 275 pounds! After the shot, he turns to me and says "You know, together with other components of the Eightfold Path we discussed earlier, I merely take the Right Action with my swing and the ball just happens to be there in the way." I've heard this before, and I think I am sort of getting it. He has hit a near-perfect draw 250 yards, landing on the left side of the fairway with a great view of the pin.

"Okay, man—even with that shorter 3-wood drive, it can *still be* birdie time!" I exclaim. Buddha's got 207 to the flag. He quietly asks for his 3-iron. He can't be too aggressive with the pin tucked strategically in the far right of the green and protected by four bunkers.

"Go for the birdie! You've hit nearly everything so solid today. A nice controlled fade will put you right into the pin," I tell him. Wrong again. With 3-iron in hand, Buddha swings, and I see his divot fly straight out ahead of the ball, indicating a square-to-square swing. The ball is hit almost dead straight, sticks, releases, and rolls to rest at the left side of the green. He avoided potential bunker trouble by not going for the pin and shorter putt. While safely on in two, he's now got a much more difficult 30-foot putt for the bird.

Buddha explains, "Yes, hitting a fade might have gotten me in closer to the pin, but I would still have had to consider the bunkers, front, side, and back of the pin. The green is pretty wide, so it was the safer shot and the wiser play. Trust me, it's not wise to get greedy. Yes, I was tempted by the circumstances, but a deeper wisdom must prevail in these situations. As we discussed a bit before, this is Right Knowledge, the true culmination of the Eightfold Path."

With a 30-foot putt coming up, by far his longest of the day, Buddha takes his 1920s hickory-shafted putter and strokes it. He is pin-high right of the cup, leaving a 3-footer for par. "I had the golden gutter a bit too far right," he comments. He putts out and then says, "Par is a fine score, and I have been rewarded for my wise choices. I wasn't greedy. I wasn't aggressive. I was patient with myself. I now come away with a sense of gratitude for the experience, including my judgment, here at 15."

I'm a tad upset and puzzled. "This was the perfect hole for you to get aggressive and get that bogey back, but you just bailed instead! You know, no guts, no glory and all that stuff."

Buddha retorts with a wry smile, "That's why I'm a scratch golfer, and you're just angry again."

I'm afraid he's right.

BUDDHA'S CORNER

During every round of golf you will be tempted by nearly
impossible or crazy shots, but a deeper wisdom must
prevail in these situations. Instead use Right Knowledge,
the true culmination of the Eightfold Path.

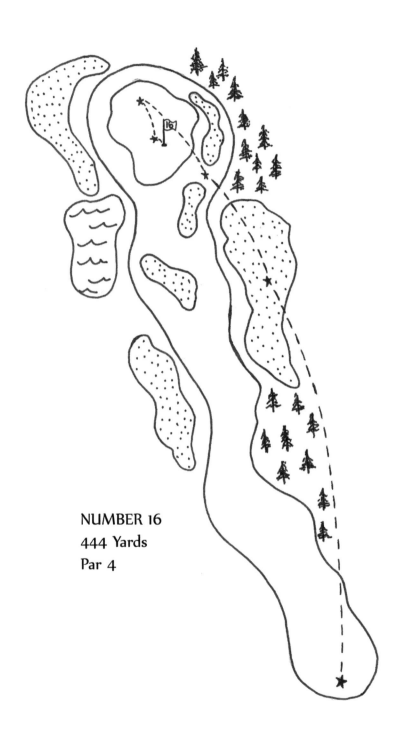

NUMBER 16
444 Yards
Par 4

NUMBER 16
444 Yards, Par 4

Caddy's View from the Tee:

Sweet 16, it's not. This is one tough par 4. Watch those massive waste bunkers, water and rough areas on both the right and left of this very narrow fairway. Two more bunkers are actually in the center of the fairway. Trees can be a real problem here too if you get over toward the fairway right edge. At the green, huge, deep sand bunkers are on the right and left. The green can be hard to hold as shots want to go left. This hole would definitely be the wrong place to get sloppy.

Buddha mis-hits his driver and sends the ball into the huge waste area bunker, right. From here he hits a high 4-iron onto the apron. For his third, he delicately pitches onto the back left of the green. Buddha again explains his children's purple wading pool visualization. "It's very important to clearly see the purple pool and stay down and steady through the shot."

Now on the green, he two-putts. With a bogey 5, this was not a model hole for Buddha, but given the potential for trouble, it could have been a whole lot worse.

"So what happened here?" I inquire.

Buddha analyzes the situation and philosophizes, "In golf, like life, events are always interrelated, constantly changing and often unpredictable. I did not properly visualize the orange stake on my downswing, and as a result, my misguided drive forced me into an almost impossible approach shot. From the right front fairway my pitch was decent, but again, this was not an easy shot. And two putts on this green wasn't really so bad because I had to fight a big right-to-left break."

He continues, "My visualizations were a bit weak on this hole, especially with my first and second shots—and it showed. I paid the price. But it's now *far more important* just to let it go and not allow the experience to rattle me. With the right attitude, I can even enjoy a less-than-great hole, so to speak, and I'll be wiser as I face the next challenge.

"It is during the disappointing moments in life and in golf that we must strive even harder to follow the Eightfold Path. In particular, on this hole, I had to get back to Right Effort, Right Thought, and Right Mindfulness. In this way one can not only play better golf but also live an exemplary life and reincarnate after death into a higher form."

"Okay—*hold it right there, Buddha!*" I interject. "Reincarnate? Does this mean that if I use Right Speech and stop swearing or lying on the golf course, and live an exemplary life using the other seven of the Eightfold Path principles, I can come back as a combination of Byron Nelson, Bobbie Jones, Ben Hogan, and Walter Hagen all- in-one?"

To that, Buddha lays *this* on me, "Well, you *are* over-simplifying things a bit, but you're not all that wrong. Let's use this nasty bogey here at 16 as an example. If one's intention is to be positive and improve from an experience, one is said to have good *karma*. If one's intention is negative and you choose to obstruct your improvement, you have bad karma. So karma has everything to do with your intention and motivation in life. Good intentions and motivations yield good karma.

"When you leave this life through death, your karma will bring you back into the world either in a higher or lower form than you are now, and not necessarily in a human form. The choice is yours. And the reincarnation cycle is continuous. So you may eventually come back as your golf dream team, or you might come back as a divot! That choice is yours."

Through reincarnation and good karma you could come back in your next life as your entire golf "Dream Team" rolled into one!

Whew! I'm contemplating all I just heard. Let me get this straight: *Reincarnation* of my golf game. So, okay, as I build and maintain good karma (through my good intentions and motivations) I may eventually come back in my next life as the golfer of my dreams. There's still hope for me in the Nirvana Golfers Hall of Fame! I feel elated.

With that last bogey, we lost a stroke and are now back to 8-under par. I pick up Buddha's bag once more, and we stroll over to Number 17.

BUDDHA'S CORNER

ON SELF-REALIZATION, KARMA, NIRVANA AND HOLES-IN-ONE

Once you are fully "self-realized" and have attained enlightenment or Nirvana, you will be so perfect that you won't even need a "physical-ness" at all. You will have transcended all that is life or golf. Then and only then will *your every shot* be a perfect hole-in-one—but even *that* won't matter anymore. You will be forever "at One" with the golf ball.

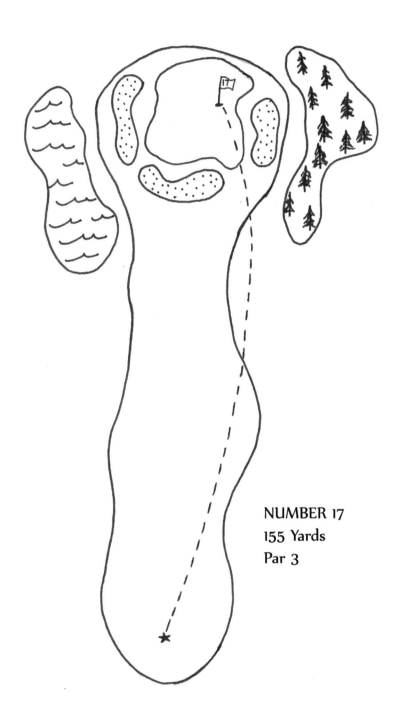

NUMBER 17
155 Yards
Par 3

NUMBER 17
155 Yards, Par 3

Caddy's View from the Tee:

This is no cream puff par 3. Sometimes it feels calm at the tee, but the flag says differently. Better be very careful. The pond to the left is in play; a dense pine forest is right; three bunkers guard the green. The fairway is comprised of a huge dip running almost its entire length.

Having already forgotten his bogey at 16, Right Thought (visualization), Right Concentration (focus) and, most importantly Right Mindfulness (being in the present moment) are on Buddha's mind. He asks for his old forged 6-iron and nails it into the headwind. A soft landing, two bounces up onto the green, rolling, breaking, slowing, still rolling—and Buddha gets a hole-in-one!

I jump with glee and congratulate Buddha profusely. He just grins and borrowing a line from Lee Trevino says, "What's the big deal—that's what I'm *supposed* to do in golf, isn't it?" I love the ever-optimistic attitude in his comment. And you know, I never really thought about a hole-in-one quite that way before!

"But how did you do it with such an old and heavy forged-head, steel-shafted iron?" I ask. "No cavity back? No graphite? No titanium? I mean that forged 6-iron blade you used is ancient."

Buddha is quick to jump on my observation, "Oh, you're confusing new with better—a common folly, I'm afraid. My forged irons are from 1983, so what? Do you judge quality by youth? I was born in 563 B.C. almost 2,600 years ago, so what does that make *me*?"

Point taken. Senior citizen Buddha moves to 10-under par with one hole left to play. His score is now bordering on the incredible, and we are close to setting a new club record.

BUDDHA'S CORNER

Don't confuse new with better. You can do great things with ancient, yet correct, thinking.

"It's in the hole!"

~Bill Murray, 1980,
Caddyshack

BUDDHA'S CORNER

Two of the most famous shots in golf history occurred at 17 at Pebble Beach, and both involved Jack Nicklaus. On the par 3 17th hole of the final round of the U.S. Open in 1972, Nicklaus hit a 1-iron into the teeth of the wind and hit the flagstick. He birdied and won the tournament.

Ten years later, also on No. 17 in the final round at Pebble Beach, Tom Watson holed out a seemingly impossible chip shot to beat Nicklaus for the U.S. Open title. Just after sinking the chip, Watson pranced across the green, pointed to his renowned caddy, the late Bruce Edwards, and proclaimed, "See—I told you I was going to hole it!"

Buddha says that both these iconic 17th hole moments from Nicklaus and Watson were superb examples of the power of visualization. It worked for them and it can work for you.

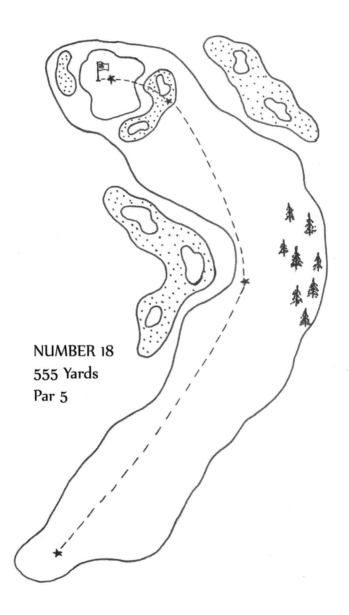

NUMBER 18
555 Yards
Par 5

NUMBER 18
555 Yards, Par 5

Caddy's View from the Tee:

Number 18 presents great beauty, opportunity and challenge, all rolled into a finishing par 5. The prevailing wind is strong here, sometimes very strong, blowing left-to-right and fighting a draw for distance shot. The huge fairway bunker to the left is definitely in play, so don't hook it; even a draw could be chancy here. At about 300 yards out a small grove of trees makes a good spot-landmark— but stay left of them or else! The approach to the green is tough, as usual, the sand bunkers menacing all around. The gateway at the front-left of the green is extremely narrow.

I don't want to jinx Buddha so I decide not to tell him that a birdie here will break the club record. Buddha goes with his driver off the tee and hits a monstrous 290-yard draw to the left of the fairway pines, landing in perfect position. As we walk out to his ball, we pass the fairway pines and Buddha reflects, "Trees have such power and beauty. They are flexible enough to bend with storms, yet remain strong and magnificent.

"Just look at the pines here on the fairway. I love and cherish trees, even as obstacles on a golf course. In fact, these beautiful pines remind me of the Bodhi tree that provided shelter for me during my meditations, which ultimately led me to supreme enlightenment. It was under the Bodhi tree when I discovered the interrelatedness of all things in life.

"The pines here on this 18th fairway are ever-changing; they are even changing incrementally right now as we walk by them. Like I said back on Number 7, nothing is ever the same, second by second. The trees here on 18 are constantly changing and *change itself* is the only reality."

115

We reach his ball. From an excellent fairway lie, he draws a 235-yard 3-wood but catches the right front greenside bunker. With no fear of sand (as he explained earlier in the round) he nonchalantly splashes out with his 56-degree sand wedge to within three feet of the pin.

He goes into his usual pre-shot routine and Eightfold Path principles. His putt is right-to-left and slightly uphill. The green is only medium-fast this later time of afternoon. After his usual golden gutter and Mercury dime putt visualizations, he rolls it in smoothly for a closing birdie.

Buddha comes in with an 11-under par 61, a new course record!

BUDDHA'S CORNER

At the Pebble Beach Pro-Am in 1984, Hale Irwin was trailing by one on the 18th tee in the final round. His tee shot was well left, heading out of bounds. His ball hit the rocks on the left shoreline—and then bounced back into the fairway! Irwin wound up with a birdie on the hole then won the tourney in a playoff.

Buddha says that you need to stay cool no matter what unexpected things happen—yes, even on Number 18 at Pebble.

After having Buddha autograph the flag for me at 18 (okay, I'll pay for a replacement flag, I promise), it seems appropriate to ask him what one thing was the most important from all we had discussed today.

Like a college professor on the last day of class, Buddha is not missing his chance to sum it all up for me. "Well," he replies, "as I originally learned under the Bodhi tree, all things are interrelated. My golf swing is a good example since there are many interrelated factors behind it. Each element of the swing by itself does not seem that complex, but putting it all together for best results takes practice—lots of practice. Don't get discouraged or impatient. Anything worthwhile in life, including scratch golf, takes practice.

"Do you think Byron Nelson was routinely scoring eagles while in kindergarten?" (Answer: No, probably just birdies.) "And do you know that Ben Hogan spent hours on the practice tee the *same night* after he had just *won* the U.S. Open? Control of the mind in a constructive, positive way is Right Effort. That in turn feeds Right Mindfulness and Right Concentration, the abilities you need to create and hold visualizations. I practice all of this in my pre-shot routines, *every* time with *every* shot.

"I strive to exercise only Right Speech by avoiding lies or deception, and I don't use profanity or even harsh words directed at my ball, even if I severely slice or hook.

"During my back swings, I employ Right Thought by keeping negative words out of my mind. I don't allow myself to think about my past less-than-perfect shots, but it takes Right Effort and Right Concentration to do that. I hold no anger. No frustration. No distraction. Not even a lust for more distance. In short, I hold no attachments at all.

"I stay in the present moment and in reality—no daydreaming about what my round today, yesterday, or tomorrow could be, might be, or should be. This is Right Mindfulness. "I perform Right Effort by putting harmonious positive energy into the golf ball at the moment of impact. There's no negativity in my mind as I swing into the ball, just a smooth, fluid, natural movement. I remember that Slammin' Sammy Snead used to talk about giving that 'little 'ol golf ball a fun ride into the sky.' This very playful and happy swing thought helped him drive the ball record distances.

"I need Right Action to stay true to myself at all times on the course—no cheating, no illegal clubs or other equipment. Honesty and my own integrity are necessities of life, not 'optional extras'. Think about that great golfer, Arnold Palmer, who is looked to as the King of Integrity.

"In answering your present question, I hope I'm performing Right Livelihood, as I consider my profession to be a teacher of philosophy. I hope that my teachings are helpful for those who choose to hear me, but I also understand that they must be *ready* to hear me.

"And finally, I continue to aspire to Right Knowledge. All the elements above need to be operating together inside my present reality. In living my life, I can't allow the essential truths to become non-practical, purely theoretical or distorted—otherwise, I will fall back into the ignorance that leads to suffering. And I must always stay focused on my goal. Ultimately, Right Knowledge leads to enlightenment or Nirvana.

"Right Effort, Right Concentration, Right Thought, Right Mindfulness, Right Action, Right Speech, Right Livelihood, and Right Knowledge are the elements of the Eightfold Path. These are the ways, the *only ways*, to eliminate golf suffering. I used them all in this round.

"The Eightfold Path is beautifully analogous to golf: To have a pure, suffering-free experience, all of the aspects of your game—mental and physical—must be present and working

together in constructive harmony, integrated into your long and challenging journey around the course."

"A vast amount of consistent practice of the Eightfold Path principles is required. You don't just wake up enlightened one day. Everything I just said applies to golf and all of life. Get it?" He winks. And with that, Buddha and I head over to the clubhouse for the 19th hole.

BUDDHA'S CORNER

ONLY AT THE HIGHEST LEVELS OF ZEN MEDITATION, YOU BECOME:

At One with your swing.

At One with your putts.

At One with your golf ball.

At One with your clubs (yes, even your driver!)

At One with the course.

At One with the winds, trees, flowers, and ALL around you.

At One with the water hazards, sand bunkers, forests, and even the out of bounds stakes.

At One with everything, everywhere!

INSIGHTS AT THE 19th HOLE

Inside the clubhouse at the Enlightenment Golf & Country Club, Buddha sits relaxing.

Let's review his record-breaking round:

HOLE	BLUE	WHITE	HDCP	BUDDHA	PAR	RED
1	406	380	6	3	4	300
2	522	490	4	4	5	420
3	404	370	10	4	4	320
4	337	327	8	3	4	310
5	190	190	16	2	3	170
6	510	470	2	5	5	410
7	110	110	18	2	3	100
8	430	400	12	4	4	335
9	490	440	14	3	4	365
OUT	3399	3177		30	36	2730
10	441	430	5	3	4	345
11	383	370	7	3	4	340
12	212	200	15	2	3	170
13	403	375	9	3	4	310
14	580	510	3	6	5	410
15	457	390	11	4	4	300
16	444	430	13	5	4	351
17	155	155	17	1	3	185
18	555	490	1	4	5	388
IN	3630	3350		31	36	2742
TO-TAL	7019	6527		61	72	5479

ENLIGHTENMENT GOLF & COUNTRY CLUB

As superb as this record-breaking round appears, it was still *not* a perfect journey. Heck, even the great Buddha bogeyed 14 and 16! But life is always imperfect, otherwise Buddha would ace everything and always shoot scores of 18! In golf and life, there are always challenges, mishaps, frustrations, hazards and unexpected changes in conditions. Buddha, using his principles, has worked to reduce his suffering, *but it took a whole lot of dedicated practice of the right stuff to get there.*

Buddha's own reflection on his great round is surprisingly minimal. Using Right Mindfulness, he truly lives only in the *here and now.* His golf round, as spectacular as it was, is now over—behind him, literally forever. He enjoyed his journey around the course and learned still more about himself through the experience. But he's not impressed with himself or the record-breaking score he just posted.

Buddha leans back in his chair and offers one last reflection, "If you live an exemplary life, you eventually will come back without a physical body at all—you won't need it."

If that's the case, I could actually set new course records without even owning any golf clubs or physically playing a round—but then again, the *really* odd thing is that I wouldn't care about my score anyway!

BUDDHA'S CORNER

RECAP OF THE FOUR NOBLE TRUTHS AND APPLICATIONS FOR YOUR GOLF GAME

 Golf is suffering. (Certainly no argument, here!)

 Your golf desires, or "attachments," continuously feed your suffering while on the course. Attachments would include—are you ready for this *brief, partial* list?

Your desires, wishes, hopes, dreams or expectations regarding perfect ball flight, long and straight drives, high and soft hybrids that hit the green, one-putts, perfect weather conditions, the newest clubs, the longest golf balls, up and down on all chips, your great scores, winning the club tournament, your scratch handicap and your jammed-full mahogany trophy case.

 Eliminate your golf attachments and you will eliminate your golf suffering. So just stop wanting all that stuff listed above! (Easier said than done, granted, but give it a try!)

 Practicing the Eightfold Path principles is *the only way out* of your suffering, in golf or life.

INSIDE BUDDHA'S GOLF BAG

DRIVER & WOODS   Swing easy—very easy! Pretend you are swinging your 8-iron, visualize, and hit down on the imaginary "orange stake." For fairway woods, unless there is major trouble long, take one club more than you think you need and swing easy. *Stop trying to murder the ball*; instead stay smooth, down and through the shot. Finish high with your belt buckle facing your target, but do it with poise and rhythm. Also, see the "orange stake" below.

HYBRIDS & LONG IRONS   Stay down and through the ball; let your club do the work. Unless there is major trouble long, as with the woods, take one more club than you think you need. Remember that long irons will generally be more accurate than hybrids, but hybrids will give you more consistent solid ball contact. *The longer the club, the more important it is that you swing easy while visualizing the orange stake.* Follow through on these longer clubs as smoothly as you can and finish high.

MID-IRONS   We're talking *accuracy* with these clubs. Don't get cute or try to play over your ability and practice level. Go for one side of the green, and pick your spot-target a few yards ahead of the ball. If you are fading or drawing the ball, spot-aim accordingly. Unless there is major trouble long, take one more club than you think you need. *On your scorecard, keep track of how many times you were short or long of the greens when you played a mid-iron.* (Buddha bets that you were short of the greens far more often than you were long!)

SHORT-IRONS & WEDGES   Stay focused. Don't start your swing until you can clearly see your visualized "children's purple wading pool" target. Change the colors of the pool if you need to in order to see it clearly in your mind. Stay down on the shot; force yourself not to look up until the ball is well airborne. If hitting from within a few yards of the green or from the apron, *stay down until you actually hear the ball gently soft land on the green—then and only then, look up.*

PUTTER *Visualization* is the key to putting! Study the line and grain; see the golden gutter and the Mercury dime and then take your putter back, slow and smooth, within the gutter. You must not just practice your putting stroke; you must also practice your visualizations as they work in harmony with your stroke for consistent putting.

BUDDHA'S MASTER LIST
of On-Course Tips to Instantly *Improve* Your Golf Scores
MECHANICS AND VISUALIZATIONS

Buddha says that for all your future rounds:

- Do yoga stretching at the practice tee before you begin; develop positive thoughts and images for your round; do deep breathing at the practice tee and at numerous times throughout your round; relax and enjoy your outdoor surroundings.

- Write mantras (reminders) on the soleplates of your woods and hybrids. Read them and focus on your swing thoughts every time you pull out the club.

- Once on the course, stand behind your ball before each shot and "see" the ball flight in your mind. Pick a spot-target about one yard in front of your ball, and carefully align to it. Be sure to check both your feet and shoulder alignments.

- On your first move down at the very start of your downswing, imagine an orange-colored stake in the ground just behind your right pants pocket. Gently "hammer" this stake into the ground with your downswing. This keeps your right shoulder "down and in" instead of "out and around" as you come into the ball.

- Swing every club like it's an 8-iron—very easy and through the ball. Swinging too hard will almost always throw your right shoulder outside the correct swing path, resulting in pulls and pull-slices.

- Finish high on full shots; just swing and let the ball get in the way. Don't "block" out shots; once you start down there's nothing you can do about it anyway, so just let go.

- Study your divots. In which direction do they point? This indicates your swing path direction into the ball (divot pointing right is a push or draw; divot pointing left is a pull, slice, duck-hook or pull-fade).

- On chips and pitches, aim for your visualized children's purple wading pool, and try to land your ball in it. Don't try to sink every chip or pitch; just get it close enough for a one putt. Try to leave uphill putts.

- No peeking on chips or putts; keep your head down and steady until you actually hear the ball hit the green.

- On putts, visualize a golden gutter and Mercury dime (or other items of your choice in which your putt will travel). Stroke your putter inside the walls of the gutter, starting your putter back within the gutter walls as well. Aim for only one-half of the hole, depending on the break. See the dime right where you want the putt to drop.

- *Never* take any swing or putting stroke without first visualizing the result you want.

Keep your ego out of your golf game. Driving distance is only one part of the game!

Just forget that last bad shot or putt. Stay in the present moment—it's all that matters!

Slow down all your thinking and actions before, during, and after your round.

BUDDHA'S MASTER LIST
of Eightfold Path Principles that Will Instantly *Improve* Your Golf Scores

BEHAVIORS & ATTITUDES
WHILE ON THE COURSE

RIGHT SPEECH

No cursing at your golf ball.
Give no advice unless asked.
No arguing.
No scolding of that slow foursome in front of you.
Call out "fore" loudly to warn others of stray shots.
No talking to distract your playing partners.

RIGHT LIVELIHOOD

Be honest and of service in earning
the money that pays for your golf.
No sandbagging of your handicap if you
are making money by competing on the course.

RIGHT THOUGHT

Always create a detailed pre-shot positive
visualization or picture in your mind.
Imagine a positive picture that is framed
in a camera viewfinder or screen—
this is important on each and every shot
and exponentially important on putts.
Right Thought also includes the correct
mechanical swing thoughts.

You must *see* success.

RIGHT EFFORT

Don't even start your backswing
until you hold only *positive* swing thoughts.
Many Hall of Fame golfers claim that
their positive mental approach to the game
was extremely important to their success.

RIGHT CONCENTRATION

Get your visualized shot image into
precise, sharp focus, and hold it there.
Think of your framed image, but
now with added razor-sharp focus.
Envision the ball going through the air, including
flight direction and altitude.

RIGHT ACTION

No cheating of any kind.
No "Mulligans." (Ouch, *that* hurts.)
No "lie improvement" in the rough.
No illegal clubs, balls or other stuff in the bag.
(Better get rid of those old deep U-grooved
wedges; they're illegal now—sorry!)

RIGHT MINDFULNESS

Stay in the present moment;
forget your previous bad shot.
Just keep practicing mindfulness and watch how
the winning pros do this, especially on Sundays.

And the culmination of all the above seven principles flow into:

 RIGHT KNOWLEDGE

Through deep meditation, '"Zen", and use
of the above principles, become at one with
your golf game and the rest of the world.

You are now a Platinum Member at the
Enlightenment Golf & Country Club!

BUDDHA'S MASTER TO DO LIST
That Will Instantly *Destroy*
Your Golf Game

Okay, we've looked at a recap of what *to* do; here's Buddha's Master List of what *not* to do. See yourself anywhere in here? If yes, re-read the appropriate sections of the book and continue to consistently practice all the mental and physical tips.

WARNING: *Frequent* use of the below 15 behaviors will almost guarantee that you will never legally break 90 in your current lifetime. As a result, you are destined to come back in your *next* lifetime yet *again* as a high-handicapper, still with much to learn!

TO *DESTROY* YOUR GOLF GAME:

 Don't practice with purpose; just hit balls for kicks once in a while.

 Don't practice or stretch before a round; just jump out of your car and head to the first tee.

 Carry a million golf balls—you already know you will need them during your round.

 Try a shot on the course that you have never practiced.

 Give unsolicited advice to playing partners.

Be rude or impatient with others on the course.

 Swear at your golf ball.

 Take Mulligans.

 Have no positive, consistent swing thoughts; just walk up and hit the ball.

 See no images of your ball in the air.

 Keep buying new equipment, always looking for the "right" driver or the "magic" putter.

 Lie about your score.

 Ignore your outdoor surroundings.

 Keep looking at your wristwatch during the round.

 Leave your cell phone on, and take all your calls during your round.

Free Golf Tips!

Now I don't hold the expectation (or Buddhist "attachment") that this little book alone will get you to the Masters at Augusta for a 1PM tee time on that sunny April Sunday. But I *can* tell you that if you *consistently practice* the mental tips, swing and putt techniques and course management behaviors within this book, you *will* see significant improvements in your game, regardless of your current level of play.

Okay, but this *is* golf after all and we all need all the on-going, continuous help we can get. In that spirit, Buddha provides *free golf tips* to our friends and followers every week at the website and through blogs, YouTube, facebook, LinkedIn and twitter, so please stay in touch with us.

**Now, go out there and totally experience
your golf journey (and life) —
and enjoy every present moment!**

Share Your Stories

In the generous spirit of Buddhist philosophy, please share your golfing experiences, visualization ideas, and success stories with fellow golfers at the following sites:

www.BuddhaPlays18.com
YouTube.com/BuddhaPlays18
facebook.com/BuddhaPlays18
LinkedIn.com/BuddhaPlays18
twitter: @BuddhaPlays18

A Quick Bio of the Buddha

Siddhartha Gautama Sakyamuni, known as "the Buddha," was born in 563 BC into royalty in an area that is now considered Nepal. His mother, Mahamaya, died eight days after he was born. His father, King Suddhodana, was afraid that Siddhartha would abandon the kingdom and kept him confined to the royal palace. At 20, Siddhartha's marriage was arranged to Princess Yasodhara.

At the age of 22, the previously confined Siddhartha finally discovered more about the outside world. He saw suffering everywhere. About this time his son, Rahula, was born. By age 23 or 24, Siddhartha left his family, his position, and the palace in search of worldly answers. This was a great sacrifice for him, but he felt compelled to travel and study the suffering in the world.

From his studies Buddha learned about the interrelationships of different aspects of life and the actual causes of suffering. From the age of about 27 on Buddha devoted his life to communicating his discoveries to the world so that others could find enlightenment. Buddha preached a middle path—behaviors that avoid extremes of either luxury or self-denial.

After many long years he returned to his home as "the Buddha," which roughly translated means "the Awakened One." His wife Yashodara then joined him, and her own life became one of devotion to the Buddhist path.

The Buddha's teaching career lasted for 45 years until his death in 483 BC. Of course, Buddha could currently hold every golf trophy in existence, but he has long since transcended his desire to do so.

Buddha's Favorite
Introductory Books on Buddhism

These superb, easy-to-read and often humorous books offer basic introductions to Buddhist philosophy:

Awakening the Buddha Within by Lama Surya Das. Broadway Books, 1997. ISBN 0-553-06695-1

How to Become a Buddha in 5 Weeks by Giulio Cesare Giacobbe, Metro Books, 2005. ISBN 978-1-4351-2053-2

The Heart of the Buddha's Teaching by Thich Nhat Hanh. Parallax Press, 1998. ISBN 0-938077-81-3

201 Little Buddhist Reminders by Barbara Ann Kipfer. Ulysses Press, 2006. ISBN 1-56975-518-3

Worlds of Harmony by the Dalai Lama. Parallax Press, 1992. ISBN 978-1-888375-81-7

The Art of Happiness by the Dalai Lama. Riverhead Books, 1998. ISBN 1-57322-111-2

Buddhism for Dummies by Jonathan Landaw and Stephan Bodian. Wiley Publishing, 2003. ISBN 978-0-7645-5359-2

Essential Buddhism by Jacky Sach. Adams Media, 2006. ISBN 1-59869-129-5

The Everything Buddhism Book by Jacky Sach. Adams Media, 2003. ISBN 1-58062-884-2

The Religions of Man by Huston Smith. Harper & Row, 1958. ISBN 0-06-080021-6

Buddha's Favorite (& Classic) Books On Golf

There are hundreds of golf instruction books and Buddha (and your author) have read nearly all of them. Most of these books tend to center on the traditionally taught, purely mechanical aspects of the golf swing, as opposed to the mental part of the game.

Below are listed, in alphabetical order by golfer's last name, some of the best "traditional" instruction books of all-time, at least in Buddha's opinion (and don't forget this old guy just shot a 61!). Buddha says that *every* serious golfer should take a look at these classics:

Ben Hogan
5 Lessons: The Modern Fundamentals of Golf. Fireside Publications, 1985.   ISBN 9780671612979.

Power Golf. Gallery Publications, 2010. ISBN 9781439195284.

Tom Kite
How to Play Consistent Golf. Pocket Books, 1994.
        ISBN 9780671510985.

Jack Nicklaus
Golf My Way (with Ken Bowden). Simon & Shuster, 2005.
        ISBN 9780743267120.

Jack Nicklaus' Lesson Tee (with Ken Bowden). Simon & Schuster, 1992. ISBN 9780671780074.

Jack Nicklaus' Playing Lessons. Golf Digest Books, 1981.
        ISBN 9780914178422.

Putting My Way (with Ken Bowden). Wiley & Sons, 2009.
        ISBN 9780470487792.

(continued)

Arnold Palmer
495 Golf Lessons. Follett Publishing, 1973. ISBN 9780695804022.

My Game and Yours. Simon & Schuster, 1984.
    ISBN 9780671471958.

Play Great Golf. Doubleday, 1987. ISBN 9780385243018.

Situation Golf. McCall Publications, 1970. ISBN 9780841500235.

Gary Player
Golf Begins at 50. Simon & Schuster, 1989.
    ISBN 9780671638610.

Tom Watson
Getting Up and Down. Random House, 1987.
    ISBN 9780394753003.

For instant access to our website, **BuddhaPlays18.com**, just scan your smart-phone over this barcode.

Smart-Phone Applications

For Yoga, try: YOGAWORKOUT by LifeApps, LCC

For Golf, try: PGA Tour, Like a Pro Free, Putting Pro, and Perfect Road.

ABOUT THE AUTHOR
Edward Sarkis Balian, Ph.D.

An avid golfer for almost 50 years, Ed Balian grew up in one of golf's golden eras featuring Hall of Fame stars no less than Arnold Palmer, Jack Nicklaus, Gary Player and countless other greats.

On Ed's first course outing at 13 years of age, he and a childhood friend, both decent golfers, were actually criticized because golf was explained to them as strictly an "old man's game." My, how things have changed—for the better!

Specializing in Palmer, Nicklaus and Player memorabilia, Ed collects vintage clubs, scorecards, flags, golf board games, vintage photos and other links items. He holds a great enthusiasm for the study and teaching of golf as he loves the never ending challenge of the game.

Ed holds a Ph.D. in Education with a minor in Social Research from Wayne State University, Detroit, Michigan. He has spent decades as an entrepreneur, business owner and university professor. Ed is a published songwriter, musician, photographer and author. He resides just north of coastal San Diego with wife, Judith. His children, Hilary, Jay (lefty golfer), Brad, and Roxanne live in the golf Nirvana states of Arizona and Hawaii.

Ed can be found regularly practicing Buddhist philosophy at the Encinitas Ranch Golf Course or at Torrey Pines Golf Course in San Diego.

To order *Buddha Plays 18*, please visit:

www.BuddhaPlays18.com
www.amazon.com
or select retail outlets.

on YouTube: BuddhaPlays18
on Facebook: BuddhaPlays18
on LinkedIn: BuddhaPlays18

Dealer inquiries welcomed at:
www.BuddhaPlays18.com

Other books by Dr. Edward Sarkis Balian and Silver Sky Publishing, USA

Buddha's 102 Golden Golf Tips

Buddha Meets the Beatles (or, He loves you, yeah, yeah, yeah!)

77 (Leadership & Life Lessons)

The Graduate Research Guidebook, 4th Edition